Art in Your World

SECOND EDITION

Gerald F. Brommer
George F. Horn

Davis Publications, Inc.
Worcester, Massachusetts

Art in Your World

SECOND EDITION

Copyright 1985
Davis Publications, Inc.
Worcester, Massachusetts U.S.A.

Graphic Design: Penny Darras-Maxwell
Cover Illustration: Diane Nelson

Printed in the United States of America

Library of Congress Catalog Card Number: 84-73493

ISBN: 0-87192-168-5

AYW—2ND. ED.

Title page: Still Life with Guitar. *Tempera painting by a student from Seoul American School, Korea.*

1991 Impression

10 9 8 7

Contents

The Value of Art in Your World   7

1 An Important Part of Your World   8
Suggested Activities   19

2 Why Artists Create   20
Fine Artists   23
Designers and Commercial Artists   24
Craftspeople   26
Suggested Activities   27

3 Art and Commerce   28
Graphic Design   29
Industrial Design   31
Fashion Design   34
Suggested Activities   35

4 Designing Your Living Space   36
Architecture   36
Interior Design   41
Landscape Design   44
Suggested Activities   45

5 The Fine Arts   46
Suggested Activities   52

Understanding Art in Your World   53

6 The Elements and Principles of Design   54
The Elements of Design   54
The Principles of Design   61
Summary   66
Suggested Activities   66

7 The History of Art   68
Ancient Times   68
The Middle Ages   72
The Renaissance   74
The Baroque and Rococo   79
The Nineteenth Century   81

Impressionism and Postimpressionism   84
The Twentieth Century   87
Contemporary Art   92
Suggested Activities   94

8 Influences in Your Contemporary Culture   96
Asian Influences   97
Blck African Influences   98
Mexican Influences   100
American Indian Influences   101
The Influence of Women   102
Other Influences on Our Culture   104
Suggested Activities   106

Creating Art   107

9 Drawing   108
Tools and Techniques   111
Some Design Suggestions   116
What Can You Draw?   118
Line   120
Shape   122
Value and Form   124
Textures and Patterns   126
Space and Perspective   129
Using Letters and Words   132
Scratching Out   134

10 Painting   138
Materials, Tools and Techniques   140
Design Suggestions   146
The Importance of Color   148
What Can You Paint?   150
Painting People Around Us   152
Painting a Still Life   156
Painting Your Environment   160
To Catch the Action   162
Using Your Imagination   164
What's New in Painting?   168

11 Printmaking 174
    Looking for Subject Matter 176
    Design Suggestions 178
    Relief Prints 180
    More Relief Prints 184
    Monoprints 186
    Experimental Prints 188

12 Sculpture 190
    Design Suggestions 194
    Modeling 196
    Clay 197
    Papier-Mâché 199
    Constructing 203
    Wire 203
    Paper and Cardboard 206
    Wood Constructions 208
    Assemblages and More 210

13 Graphic Design 212
    The Poster 212

Properties of a Poster 212
Designing a Poster 214
Specific Appeal 221
Open Space and Simplicity 221
Lettering 222
Color 223
Completing Your Poster 224
Variations 225

14 Crafts 226
    Design Suggestions 227
    Jewelry 229
    Clay 233
    Fiber Arts 239
    Summary 247

Glossary 248
Index 253
Acknowledgements 256
Picture Credits 256

How to Use This Book

Art in Your World can be adapted to suit many different teaching styles and types of curricula. It contains numerous ideas, concepts and techniques. These will stimulate teachers *and* their students. Whether you study a single section, or several, this book will spur students to learn. At the same time it will help readers become more fully aware of the art all around them.

Several important areas are emphasized: careers in art; art as expression; the structure and language of art; the history of art; art influences on our culture; and the making of art. Any or all of these can be studied in depth or used as motivation for creating art. Teachers will find that they can use this book yet schedule their programs according to their own needs and available time.

Many museums and contemporary artists have shared their work so that we can learn from their excellent examples. Teachers and students also have generously provided an extremely wide range of expression. These works of art are not intended to be copied. They should serve as examples of style, subject and concept. Individual expression is important and valuable. This book is designed to encourage awareness, creativity and sound judgment.

Art in Your World is simply examples of art from around the world, collected to make us aware of the importance of art in our daily lives and as a means of sharing and expressing our ideas.

The Value of Art in Your World

Raspberries and Goldfish, *1981, by Janet Fish is a large oil painting on canvas, 72" × 64" (182 × 162 cm). Courtesy Robert Miller Gallery, New York.*

1 An Important Part of Your World

Some people think of art as only paintings, sculptures, prints and craft objects displayed in museums and galleries. In fact, art is a part of all aspects of life. You can see the work of artists and designers wherever you look.

Your colorful breakfast cereal box, the patterns in the cloth in your home, the machines, furniture and tableware that you use each day were given their shape and form by designers.

Automobiles, bicycles and jets began on the drawings boards of stylists and industrial designers.

We do not think of seeing art in the supermarket, but artists design all the packages we find there. Graphic designers plan the decorations, logos, labels, color, type, lettering and illustrations.

This model looks like a real car, but it is actually painted clay. It was made by industrial designers to test consumer reaction. Ford Motor Co.

The world around us is full of the work of artists. This truck was designed by industrial designers and decorated by graphic artists. The 3M logo and the advertisement on the bus bench are the work of graphic designers. The building was designed by an architect.

The table, chairs, dishes, napkins and place mats were all designed by artists. The photograph was taken by a commercial photographer. Courtesy Scan, Baltimore.

*Sculptor Kent Ullberg was commissioned to create a 15'
(4.5 m) work for this interior space in the Corpus Christi
National Bank in Texas.* Watermusic *was done in polished stainless steel and black granite. Architects, interior
designers, industrial designers, lighting designers and
landscape architects also worked with this space.*

*Page layouts for magazines, books and brochures are
sketched and designed by graphic artists and book
designers.*

Your home and school, and other buildings in your
town, were designed before they were built. Many
rundown areas have been replaced with new buildings that have walkways, green areas, fountains and
sculptures. These are the work of architects and environmental planners.

The advertisements you see are planned by graphic
designers. The shows you watch have sets developed
by scenic designers. The pages of this book were laid
out by a book designer. The typeface you are now
reading was first drawn and designed by a type designer. All around you, you can see work done by
fashion designers and interior designers.

Fine art, such as sculptures and paintings, often is
housed in museums and galleries. This kind of artwork can also be found in homes, offices and outdoor areas. Perhaps your town has sculptures in a
park or murals on a large building.

Glass buildings often reflect their immediate environment. The reflections may include much older structures.

Study this shopping area and make a list of objects, concepts and graphics that were designed by specialized
artists.

You can see that art is not *only* a painting in a museum. Art is an important part of your daily life—at home, in school, in your community. Look more closely at your environment. Look above, below and around you, at home, on the streets and throughout all the areas you see each day. Look everywhere!

The next chapter will explain the differences between commercial artists and fine artists. They have similar abilities and skills. They often have different working methods and means of earning a living.

Art is the product of artists who plan and design what they do. Nature is full of design, too: the delicate pattern of veins in a leaf; the lacy design of a snowflake; the many colors and forms of flowers; the contrast of white clouds against blue sky; the many textures of tree bark; the pattern of waves against a sandy beach; the shapes of reflections; and the many patterns and textures of animal hides and bird feathers. Much human art is based on designs found in nature.

Sculptures are often used in open spaces to add color and excitement. This painted steel form by Mary Ann Miss brightens a Boston plaza.

Many historically important artworks are preserved and displayed for us in museums.

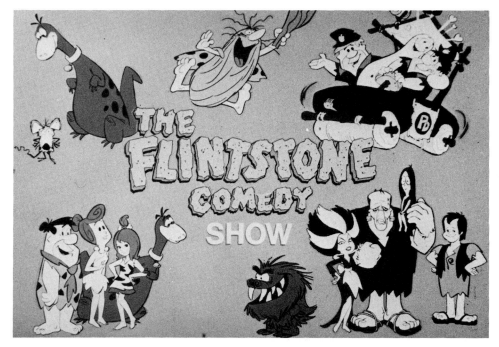

Some artists today do not use brushes, paint or chisels. This young designer is using a computer to draw. The computer image can be put into any position and permanently recorded on a printout. The computer equipment is also the product of various industrial designers.

Comic characters for television, movies and newspapers are produced by artists and studios. They help us take a different look at our environment and society. Hanna Barbera, Inc.

Flowers and leaves are only a few of nature's designs that artists have used in their art. Flower and leaf shapes are organic, interesting to use and varied. Their colors are stimulating. This black ceramic plate was designed and made by Maria Martinez. The leaf design was made by a student who used markers to create a linear pattern.

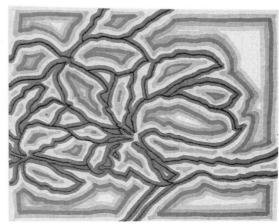

Sculptor Kent Ullberg is shown here in his studio with the clay model for Wind in the Sails. *The piece was later to be cast in bronze. He used swordfish for models and designed two beautiful, interacting forms.*

As you search for a more complete understanding of art, this book will cover many different kinds of art. It will acquaint you with the visual elements of design: *line, shape, form, space, color, value* and *texture*. You will also begin to understand the principles of design: *balance, unity, contrast, pattern, emphasis, movement*, and *rhythm*.

This text will also invite you into the world of the artist: the painter, sculptor, printmaker, architect, designer and craftsperson. It will tell you about some of the many careers in art. You will see our cultural heritage and something of the history of art. It will help you understand how events in our culture influence art and artists.

In addition, this book will help you understand art tools, materials, techniques and processes. You will use these to create your own art. You will be encouraged to express your own ideas with a variety of art materials.

Begin your study of art now. Carry a sketch pad with you. Each day, make quick sketches and notes of interesting things you see. If you have a camera, photograph scenes or objects that attract your attention. These activities will make you more aware of your visible surroundings: trees, towers, telephone poles, flowers, fences, storefronts, people, animals, trucks, cars, buses, colors, textures, shapes and forms. Collect *impressions* of things you see. You will collect ideas that you may use later for your own paintings, sculptures, prints, posters and crafts.

As you *look* and sketch what you see, you will discover the presence of art in your world. You will understand art's dynamic importance.

Artists try to communicate their personal views through their art. These three artists have individual ways of representing women in sculpture. Duane Hanson molded Lady with Coupons (far left) from polyvinyl. He painted it with oils before using actual clothing to finish his Super-Realistic form. Joel Edwards used stoneware for the figures of Two Nuns (left). He started the ceramic forms on a wheel, adding and carving as needed. The pieces were stained, not glazed, before the final firing. Henry Moore carved his abstract Broken Figure from black marble. This stylized figure represents Moore's personal artistic style.

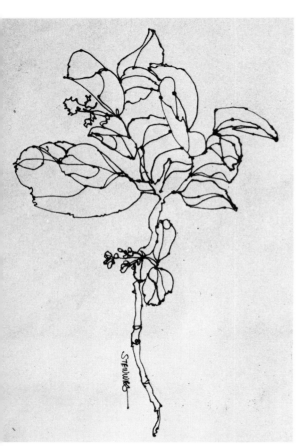

Sketchbooks are perfect places to make both visual and verbal notes about your environment. The top book contains a student's sketches of an ice cream scoop and some bird concepts. Artists never stop working in their sketchbooks. Nationally-known artist Robert E. Wood's sketchbook (lower) contains sketched impressions of people waiting for a ferry boat in Jamaica.

Suggested Activities

1. Go for a very slow walk. Stop at least every hundred feet to *look carefully* at things around you. Look at small things and large things. Look at living things and things people have made.
2. Look carefully at your environment on your way to school. Every day for a week, make a list of ten things you see that were designed by people who used artistic abilities. You can list graphic designs or manufactured objects.
3. Each day for a week make a drawing of one natural object and one manufactured object.
4. If you have a camera, take it with you on a brief walk. Use one complete roll of film to capture interesting arrangements of light and shadow. Try this with color film *and* with black-and-white film.

2 Why Artists Create

Why do some people play softball? Why do some sing songs? Work in gardens? Go for long walks along the beach? Because that is what they enjoy. Many people carve wood, mold clay, paint watercolors, design furniture because that is what they want to do most.

Why do some people type letters? Sweep floors? Sell clothes? Drive buses or trucks? Because it is their job. They are doing it because it is part of their work. For many people, art is a job, too. They may be designers, craftspersons, painters, architects or other artistically skilled workers. Their jobs use their creative abilities. They receive assignments, as you do in art class. Often they carry out their assignments in their own styles and techniques.

Different kinds of artists produce artwork for different purposes. *Fine artists* create paintings, drawings, sculptures and prints to communicate a visual message. They want us to know how they see and feel about certain subjects, ideas, scenes or people.

Designers and *commercial artists* work for other people or companies. They design the products, buildings, spaces, clothing and advertisements which surround us.

Craftspeople design and create usable objects. Their materials may include ceramics, glass, metal, wood or textiles. Their products are for sale. The public purchases craft items for their usefulness or for their beauty.

Fine artists, designers, commercial artists and craftspeople all create art of one type or another and

Fine artist Sargent Johnson created his sculpture of lacquered cloth over wood to express a deep and personal feeling. He titled it Forever Free. *Courtesy San Francisco Museum of Modern Art.*

20

The architectural firm of I. M. Pei designed the East Building of the National Gallery of Art in Washington, D.C. Hundreds of different artists developed the concept, making necessary plans and drawings, designing the interior and exterior spaces and supervising all stages of the development. More art people constantly arrange art displays and carry out the functions of such a large museum.

Otto Natzler has crafted a beautiful form that might be used for holding dried flowers or weeds. But the glaze and the form give the object its own beauty, regardless of its use. Courtesy Louis Newman Gallery.

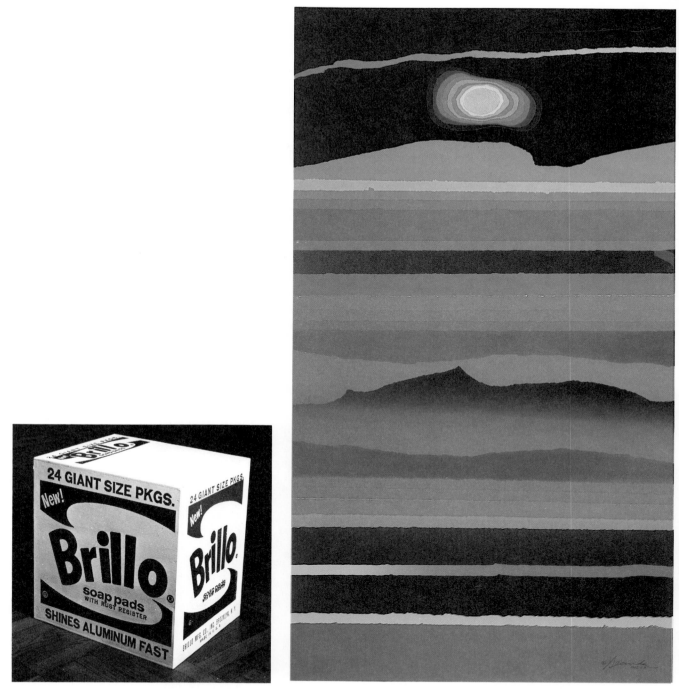

Some artists want to comment on society's problems. Andy Warhol makes us aware of our commercial environment as he produces greatly enlarged packages, such as this 17" × 17" × 14" "Brillo." Courtesy of Leo Castelli, Inc., New York.

Arthur Secunda has a unique way of expressing his feelings about his environment. In his collage, The Alps, he cut and tore colorful papers to create a visual interpretation of a special part of France.

hope to sell it to make a living. But the types of artwork they make, the reasons they make it and their methods of selling it are quite different.

Fine Artists

Art is an individual accomplishment. It begins as an idea and is complete as a viewed item. Artwork can be a unique, visible statement from the artist's inner voice. In an age of impersonal computerization and mass production, this individual statement is rare and wonderful. It is something to be valued.

The voice of the artist is in the work produced. Fine artists communicate personal responses. They show us their likes and dislikes, their impressions of beauty and ugliness, happiness and sorrow. Artists may encourage, warn, entertain or amuse us. They may shock, confuse, soothe or lift our feelings. They make statements about their religion or share special and private places.

Artists help us see and experience color and shape, form and line, lightness, darkness and space. They bring us the beauty of form and texture. Artists help us see life and objects in a new way.

All artists have this desire to say something. Poets and authors communicate with words. Composers communicate through music. Artists use visual language to present their views, to tell their stories and create their artwork.

Creating art is a process of searching, finding and telling. You *search* by looking at everything and experimenting with materials and subjects. Then you *find* a new idea of yourself, your environment and your abilities. You *tell* about your discoveries by making new artwork in your own way.

Fine artists often sell their work through galleries and agents. Sometimes they work on commission for individuals, families or companies.

Portrait artists work on commission. They are contacted by a person who wants to have a portrait painted. John Singer Sargent painted Portrait of Mrs. Edward L. Davis and her Son, Livingston Davis *as lifesize figures. Courtesy of the Los Angeles County Museum of Art (Frances and Armand Hammer Purchase Fund).*

Designers and Commercial Artists

When we hear the word "artist," we generally think of fine artists. They create artwork in private studios. Not all artists earn a living this way. There are thousands of artists who are not at all involved in creating paintings, sculptures and other such works of art.

Some designers and commercial artists started with art classes in junior and senior high school. They developed their artistic skills and interests for the business world. They saw that they could combine love of art and a lifelong career.

Designers and commercial artists sell their talents, ideas and products to earn a living. They work for other people. These artists may be involved in designing and manufacturing products. They may devise ways to advertise products. They provide artistic services which create more pleasing environments, clothing, films, books, automobiles and electronic games. They are often required to develop products from other peoples' ideas, as well as from their own.

Designers and commercial artists include architects, interior designers, graphic and industrial designers and art directors. In their jobs, business and art interact. These artists are involved with ideas, advertisements and products that affect us all. They love art and have chosen to earn a living by working with art.

Industrial designers need to know about materials and fabrication as well as design and color. This drawing shows the form of a proposed home video camera as well as its design specifications.

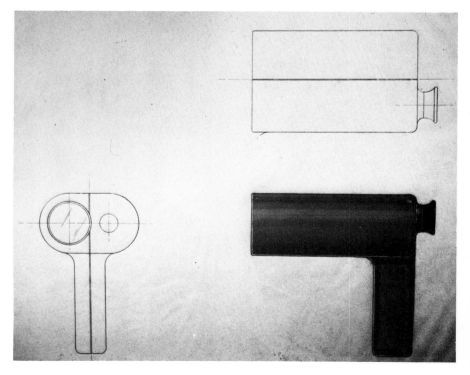

The art director in this studio is working with two graphic designers. Under his direction, they will carry out an advertising campaign. Their jobs require abilities such as drawing, visualization of ideas, layout techniques, lettering, drafting and knowledge of the use of color.

Interior designers help clients arrange their living or working areas. Some projects involve simply selecting the right chair or wall covering. Others require the complete design and furnishing of elaborate dining rooms.

Sam Maloof makes handcrafted furniture from walnut and other hard woods. His skill is much admired by other woodworkers. This cradle-cabinet combination is both useful and beautiful. Collection of Joseph Gatto.

Craftspeople

The crafts are usually separated from the fine arts, because crafts products are made to be used rather than simply enjoyed for their beauty. Some crafts products are so aesthetically pleasing, however, that their creators are clearly fine artists.

Generally the crafts include work in ceramics, glass, fabrics, metal, fiber arts and book design. In earlier days, communities relied on artisans because they designed and made all the needed utensils, clothing and tools (see the San Ildefonso water jar).

Craftspeople still produce such objects, often using old techniques. But today factories turn out most of our necessary tools and products. Artisans may create some necessary objects for themselves, for friends or for sale.

Owners of handcrafted objects may use them as intended (as dishes, pots, windows, clothing, tools, furniture, jewelry and so on). Or they may buy craft objects simply for their beauty.

An Indian artisan from San Ildefonso Pueblo (New Mexico) crafted this water jar. It was made simply to be a useful utensil. But, its form and decoration are designed so well, it can also be appreciated as a beautiful object. Courtesy The Indian Art Center of California, Studio City.

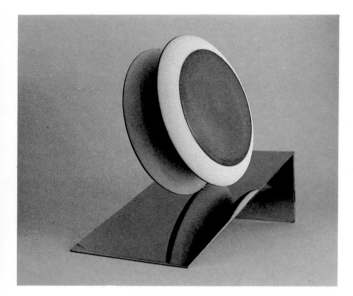

Harrison McIntosh is well known for his useful ceramic forms (bowls, jars, vases). But in this piece he has combined ceramic forms with chrome-plated steel to produce a sculptural work. Courtesy Louis Newman Gallery.

Joseph Gatto combined gold and two antique seals to create a dramatic man's ring. Traditional crafts, such as jewelry making, often demonstrate the crative abilities of individual artisans.

Craftspeople usually enjoy the creative process and the products they create. They may sell their work from their studio, through galleries and at fairs. Some artisans also teach their craft. Some work for other artisans who produce crafts in large quantities. In these ways craftspeople earn a living from their craft.

In the following three chapters you will study many kinds of art. You will learn how artists create products for the commercial, industrial and fine arts.

Suggested Activities

1. Gather examples of fine arts, crafts and commercial art from magazines. Arrange a notebook or bulletin board display. Be prepared to explain why artists create particular kinds of artwork.
2. Visit a crafts or painting studio. Ask the artist about his or her daily routine. Invite an artist or craftsperson to visit your class for a question and answer session.
3. Talk with your school's art teacher and gather student examples of fine arts, crafts and commercial arts. Display these in your classroom, and label according to the three divisions discussed here.
4. Study one craft at your school or public library. Write a brief report on the craft's history and current use.

3 Art and Commerce

Look around you! All the human-made things you see (and that is *everything* except what is in nature) have been planned by designers. Visit a shopping mall and you will see thousands of items that artists designed.

Items as small as a pencil and as tall as a high-rise building have to be designed. Clothing, books, furniture, automobiles and roller skates do not just happen. They are designed, planned and marketed for us to purchase. This is the world of commerce, and artists who design the products we use are called *commercial artists*. They work for manufacturers or design firms. Free-lance (self-employed) commercial artists work for several clients, such as company design directors or studios.

Commercial artists include: graphic designers, industrial designers and fashion designers. Artists who wish to work in these fields usually attend an art school or college. After graduating, they work for experienced designers or production companies.

There are many career specialties within each major design area. You may envision yourself in one of these jobs.

This display of equipment by LeSportsac involved a wide range of commercial artists: architect *(the building itself);* lighting designer *(the light fixtures);* industrial designer *(tracklighting system, standing lights, display fixtures);* interior designer *(floor and wall treatments, color scheme, overall coordination);* graphic designer *(titles for film presentation, labels, logos);* film art director *(film being shown on screen as part of the display);* display designer *(concept for the presentation); and the* product designer *(LeSportsac equipment).* Fabric, carpet *and* wall materials designers *were also involved.*

Photograph by Carl Furuta.

Graphic Design

Graphic designers use symbols, pictures, colors and text to attract our attention and provide information. They want their work to be beautiful, but they are judged by how effective their designs are for business. To be successful, their work must *attract* and *inform* us.

Graphic designers make printed materials attractive. They may design posters and stationery. Newspapers and magazines rely on graphic designers for advertisements, page layouts, illustrations, organization and preparation for printing. They design brochures, logos, books, packages, alphabets, containers, labels, record covers and much more.

Such artists also create television and film credits, station identifications, and some video-electronic sequences. Their tools include everything from pencils to brushes to computers.

A partial list of careers in graphic design will help you understand the range of specialists involved in commercial art.

Art Director—manages design programs
Graphic Designer—works with type and illustrations

Graphic designers are discussing the overall design for a Pro Bowl project. The art director is presenting artists' ideas for the program cover, magazine and newspaper ads, flyers, brochures, press releases, tickets, T-shirts, presentation packets and assorted symbols and identification tags. Once the concepts are approved, the production can begin.

29

Comic Strip Artist, Roger Armstrong

Type Designer—designs alphabet styles for printing

Computer Graphics Designer—uses computers to create images

Layout Artist—plans page designs

Paste-up Artist—prepares pages for printers

Letterer—hand letters signs and headings

Calligrapher—creates fancy lettering

Outdoor Advertising Designers—plans billboards and kiosks

Record Jacket Designer—creates designs for all types of records

Greeting Card Designer—executes artwork in many styles

Sign Painter—paints hand-lettered signs

Illustrator—creates artwork for many kinds of printed materials

Title Designer—designs film and television titles

Book Designer—chooses type styles, designs covers and page layouts

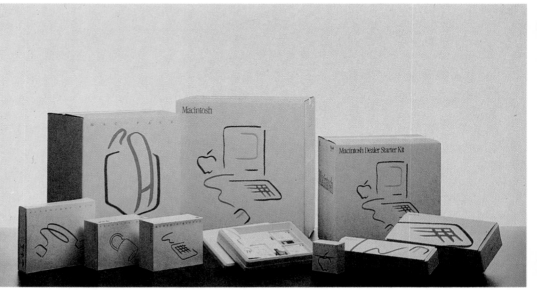

Package Designer

Courtesy of Apple Computer, Inc.

An industrial designer developed the concept of a large vehicle to haul new cars. This one is from Ford Motor Company's design department.

Cartoonists and Comic Strip Artists
Magazine Art Director—designs covers and page layouts
Teacher of Design—instructs at colleges and art schools

Industrial Design

Industrial designers plan the shapes of products such as furniture, machinery and appliances. They work with three-dimensional forms and oversee the design process from concept to packaging. They are concerned with how a product looks and how well it works. Many believe that "form follows function." A chair is something for us to sit on (a function), and something we look at (a form). First, it must be useful and comfortable. Then it must have an attractive appearance.

Sometimes industrial designers create new and exciting products. Other times their work is more practical, such as designing an automated teller for a bank. The designer determines the machine's functions and form. The machine must do all the needed banking work *and* be attractive to customers.

The automated ReadyTeller *was designed for the Security Bank system. Each part of the unit has separate functions, but they all must work together and provide a unified look. Notice all the built-in directions and instructions. The projecting blue line helps unite the components.*

31

Communications Designer, Ampex Video

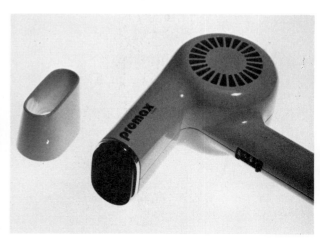

Product Designer, Robert Peterson Design

Industrial designers are responsible for all the things used in school: pencils and pens, brushes, machines, furniture, fixtures and equipment.

If you like to work with sculpture and build three-dimensional objects, perhaps you would be interested in a career in industrial design. Some typical careers include:

Toy Designer—plans toys of all types
Package Designer—designs boxes and packing crates
Product Designer—plans product forms for manufacturers
Furniture Designer—creates comfortable and handsome furniture designs
Communication Designer—designs telephones, computers
Automobile Designer—plans exteriors and interiors for cars
Airline Interior Designer—designs seats and galleys
Drafter—draws plans for construction
Lighting Designer—creates forms of lamps and light systems

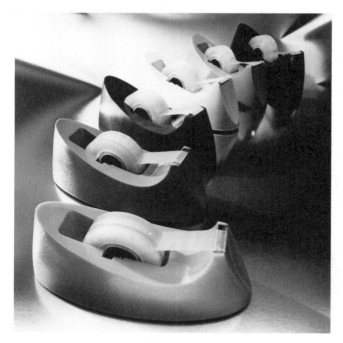

Product Designer, 3M Company

Operational Instructions:

1. To call – touch characters that correspond to the number you wish to call.
2. To terminate call – touch character marked TERMINATE.
3. For Information – touch character marked INFORMATION.
4. Emergency – touch character marked OPERATOR.

Industrial designer Robert Peterson has produced a working model of a free phone. There are no moving or loose parts exposed. It is activated by touch only. Both speaker and receiver are self-contained.

Charles Gibilterra is a free-lance furniture designer. He works for many of the best furniture manufacturers. This leather and chrome steel chair is a prototype of those to be made in a company shop.

This futuristic sports car looks like it is ready to roll, but is only a painted wood and clay model. Some day the Firebird IV may roll from Pontiac's assembly lines.

33

Boutique owners often display fashions that appeal to only a few people. Some even design clothes for special clients.

Model Maker—creates models for all kinds of products
Sports Equipment Designer—designs tennis racquets, baseball gloves, etc.
Tool Designer—plans tools used to make other products
Transportation Designer—designs trucks, buses, trains
Housing Industry Designer—designs windows, doors, sinks
Appliance Designer—plans forms of toasters, refrigerators, etc.
Medical Instrument Designer—designs machines needed by hospitals

Fashion Design

Fashion is one of the largest industries in the nation. People spend more than 100 billion dollars each year on clothing, accessories and jewelry. Because fashion trends are always changing, the future of the industry seems secure.

Top designers are the best known people in the fashion industry. They are aided by many fashion illustrators, photographers, and models; textile, jewelry and accessory designers; men's, women's, and children's clothing specialists: textile and pattern-making technicians; apparel production managers; fashion buyers and merchandisers; advertising specialists, fashion editors and writers. There are many factory workers who make the clothes, too. All of these people work together to design, manufacture, advertise and sell the clothes we wear.

Colleges and special fashion institutes offer courses in all areas of fashion design.

Some typical careers in fashion include:

Fashion Designer—creates new styles and details
Fashion Illustrator—draws fashions for ads

Fashion Photographer—photographs fashions

Accessory Designer—designs purses, belts, jewelry, etc.

Fashion Consultant—assists department store buyers

Art Director—oversees artwork created for fashion and ad agencies

Fabric Designer—plans fabrics of all types

Fashion Copywriter—writes ad copy for publications

Display Director—creates displays in stores

Fashion Editor—chooses fashion content for newspapers and magazines

Merchandising—sells fashion products

Fashion Specialist—assists in wedding and photo planning

Sports Clothes Designer—creates styles for active-wear

You can study more about fashion design by looking at many of the fashion magazines available in supermarkets and bookstores.

Suggested Activities

1. Pick one of the three major areas of commercial design (graphic, industrial or fashion) and select good examples from magazines. Write labels that explain what the designers did and arrange a display panel.
2. Walk through a shopping area. Photograph several interesting examples of graphics, industrial and fashion design. Some store managers may help you select products to photograph. Be sure to ask for permission.
3. Improve the design of an advertisement, small appliance, or piece of clothing. Sketch the new product. Write a brief description of your product. Emphasize its benefits.

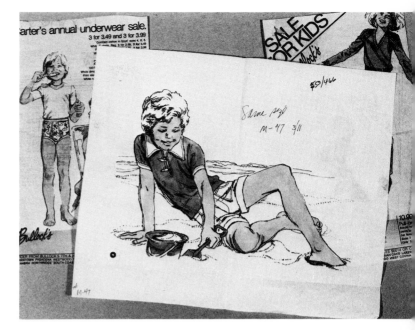

Fashion illustrator Corrine Hartley specializes in drawing children's fashions for newspaper advertisements. The drawing above will appear in ads like those seen underneath.

Fashion designers plan their designs on paper, but often work with fabrics to make examples of items they are developing.

4 Designing Your Living Space

This chapter is about art careers and space. It is *not* about rockets or astronauts though outer space equipment also is the product of many creative designers. In this chapter we look at the space around us, our own environment.

Our environment can be divided into two categories. These are the natural environment and the human-made environment. The natural environment is the space that nature has provided for us. This includes mountains, plains, water, plants and air. The human-made environment consists of everything that we have created. This includes bridges, buildings, highways, automobiles, lights and so on. It also includes the parts, such as bricks, boards, metals and glass.

Landscape architects try to use natural elements to enhance our cities. Environmental designers such as architects and interior designers use manufactured products to create the enclosed spaces in which we live.

Architecture

Buildings begin with the ideas and sketches of architects. Many other people add their ideas before the buildings are finished. Architects coordinate all the design activities. Architects make sure that *use, construction* and *appearance* are well planned.

36

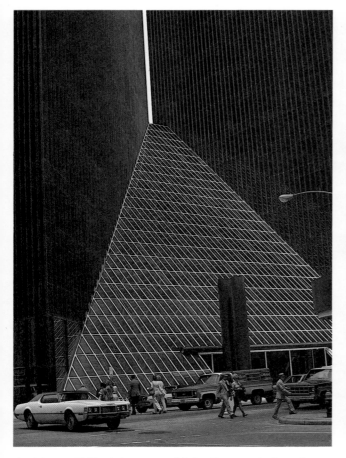

Architects Philip Johnson and John Burgee designed a unique, triangular lobby area for Houston's Pennzoil Place. The interior and exterior effects are quite different, but both add excitement to the environment.

The John Hancock Center in Chicago was designed by the architectural firm of Skidmore, Owings and Merrill of New York. Its zig-zag trim actually supports the gently tapering structure. The decorative stonework of a neighboring building provides interesting contrasts.

Use refers to the intended function of the buildings. Houses should shelter families. Office buildings must be comfortable, well-organized spaces. Theaters, churches, shopping malls and manufacturing plants all must fulfill particular requirements.

Construction refers to the physical parts of the buildings: windows, walls, ceilings, air conditioning and foundations. Architects are concerned with how these parts affect the look and usefulness of buildings.

Appearance refers to how the finished buildings will look. Do they fit in with the general environment? Are they pleasing to look at? Do they reflect the taste and quality of the community?

37

Buildings in the older areas of San Antonio (above) and San Francisco (below left) were saved by creative planners and architects who made their cities look better and restored rundown areas.

On small projects (single family homes, for example) an architect may work alone. But as projects grow in size (apartments, condominiums, multi-purpose complexes or high rise structures) more people are involved. Architectural firms employ dozens of specialists who are expert at certain phases of architectural work (drawing, planning, engineering, decorating, landscaping). The chief architect then becomes a coordinator, directing the creative activities of many.

Some of the special careers involved with architecture include:

Delineator—paints pictures of proposed buildings
City Planner—guides urban development
Environmental Designer—plans entire city areas
Drafter—draws detailed plans

This architectural plan is a watercolor painting that provided a preview look at the reception area of New York's Palace Hotel, even before its foundation was dug. The architects were Emery Roth and Son.

Architectural Graphic Artist—designs signs and logos

Model Builder—creates models of structures, areas

If you are interested in architecture as a career, you may wish to study the pictures and plans in magazines such as *Home* , *Better Homes and Gardens*, *House and Gardens* , *American Home* .

Besides designing new buildings, architects are also involved in renovating historic buildings. Some architects specialize in saving historic structures or entire sections of cities. In this way architects provide continuing reminders of our artistic heritage as well as contributing anew to contemporary culture. Perhaps your class can make a field trip to such an area in your own city or in a nearby urban area.

This dramatic design in wood and glass takes advantage of a hillside view.

Some architects' projects do not involve living or office spaces. Marcel Breuer designed the Forebay Dam and Grand Coulee Third Powerplant as part of the Columbia Basin Project in Washington. Notice the effective use of the patterns in the concrete surface.

Architects design and shape our urban environments. Their creative ideas are woven into the look and feel of our communities.

Commercial interior designer Linda Umgelter provided plans for the materials, colors, lighting, counters and physical arrangement of this Phoenix department store.

Interior Design

Interior designers plan the design and use of interior spaces. Interior decorators, on the other hand, decide colors and fabrics and the arrangement of furniture in existing spaces.

Creative interior designers make interior environments comfortable, useful and beautiful. They work with two types of clients: residential (homes, apartments and condominiums) and commercial (stores, offices, hotels, terminals and other public spaces).

Interior designers must have a good sense of design. This improves with training and experience. In addition, successful interior designers understand and work with their clients to find the best solutions to design problems.

When interior designers show clients how the finished project will look, they often make interior renderings in watercolor, pencil or markers. This one is by Said Mehrinfar of M and M Designs, in Los Angeles.

Interior designers must know about the materials with which they work. Furniture, carpets, wall coverings, fabrics, lighting fixtures, doorknobs and artwork must be chosen with care. Some items must be custom-made. Designers need to know where and how this is done.

Both designers and decorators use presentation boards to show clients the types of furniture and accessories the designer has in mind. Color swatches for paint, textile samples for furniture and carpet, tile and wood samples for floors are also presented to clients. This gives them a good idea of the look and feel of the proposed interior.

There are many specialized areas in the interior design field. Interior rendering, drafting, color styling, photography, sketching and interior illustration are only some of them. Designers may choose to work in a design studio or free-lance for many such studios.

You may enjoy seeing the work of interior designers in magazines such as *Architectural Digest, American Home, Interior, Interior Designs, Design West, Better Homes and Gardens.*

This bank counter system was designed specifically for one installation in Chicago by Robert Peterson Design. The ceiling, wall treatment, floors and lighting are part of the interior design package.

The interior design of this home uses the warm colors of the desert. Steve Chase and Associates coordinated furniture, floor coverings, accessories, wall colors and art to create a unified and unique interior environment.

Landscape Design

Landscape architects use natural elements (trees, grass, bushes, flowers, water) to design outdoor areas for buildings, highways and parks. They work alone on small projects but, more often, with architects, engineers and environmental planners on large projects.

Landscape architects' designs must be attractive and lasting. They must take into consideration the climate, soil, land contours and drainage. They also try to take advantage of the view, wind direction for cooling and sun for natural light and solar power.

Some landscape architects design the yards of fine homes. Others specialize in golf courses, shopping malls or entire urban areas. Although some landscape architects work in rural areas, most work in cities.

A landscape architect designed the area around the American Can Company building in Greenwich, Connecticut. The architect worked for the architectural firm of Skidmore, Owings and Merrill.

Landscape architects also help create beautiful and challenging golf courses. Often, the area only needs to be changed a little bit for spectacular results. But in deserts and rocky terrain, landscape architects are necessary for a successful project.

Suggested Activities

1. If a building is being constructed in your neighborhood, chart its progress by taking pictures or making notes. This is, of course, a long range project. Make a presentation when the project is completed.
2. Cut out a selection of exciting interior designs from several magazines listed in the section on interior design. Arrange a display of the best and write your own captions.
3. Pick a building in your community that could be redesigned, redecorated or updated. Photograph it and sketch your ideas for changing it.

4. Environmental planners are interested in the overall quality of our environment. Form an environmental committee with several classmates to map a problem area in your community. Make suggestions for improvement, modifications, landscaping and rehabilitations. If you furnish sketches or written ideas, a civic organization may be interested in your plan.
5. Make a floorplan of your room or another room in your home. Using a scale or 1″ = 1′, cut furniture shapes and design several arrangements for the room. You may even wish to introduce new furniture. Looking at floor plans in magazines will help.

5 The Fine Arts

We have seen how people who have different interests can have careers in art. But how do painters, sculptors and printmakers fit into the new world of computers and plastics? How do they compete? Can fine artists still communicate their ideas through traditional art forms. Can they earn enough to live by making paintings, sculptures or prints?

It would be ideal for artists to earn comfortable livings by creating art. But such situations are rare. The field is very competitive and most artists must also do other work (teaching, designing or even unrelated occupations) in order to survive.

Fine artists exhibit their work in galleries, at fairs or street sales where it can be seen and perhaps purchased by the public. This happens most often in art galleries.

Museums occasionally buy the works of outstanding artists for exhibits or permanent collections. If you want to see what today's artists are producing, go to art galleries or museums, or read about them in art magazines or books.

Kent Ullberg used a traditional subject and casting technique with new materials (polished stainless steel and red granite) to create his Lincoln Center Eagle. *The huge work is 23' (7m) high and located in Dallas, Texas.*

Dong Kingman paints ordinary subjects with a unique and personal style. In Fishing Boats on Li River, Guilin, watercolor, 22" × 30" (56 × 76 cm) his Chinese heritage is evident in both subject and technique.

The unique paintings of Nanci B. Closson reflect her interest in design and structure. The abstract elements are carefully located and painted with acrylics. Collaged papers are also added. Post Fabrication is 30" × 22" (76 × 56 cm).

Robert Vickrey has developed a powerful, personal style with egg tempera, one of the oldest mediums. Kim from Above is painted on a 30″ × 40″ (76 × 102 cm) gessoed panel.

Colleen Browning uses a traditional medium (oil) and subject matter (still life), to create a contemporary and exciting feeling. Kitchen Garden is 36″ × 50″ (92 × 130 cm). Courtesy Kennedy Galleries, New York.

The historical, cultural, ethnic and personal experience of each artist is different. Their art reflects these differences. Honest and sincere artists create to satisfy themselves. Some are *traditional* (influenced more by working methods of the past). Others blend several styles. Still others are *avant-garde* (using any and all new ways of working).

Traditional artists follow styles and techniques used by generations of artists. They become excited when working with textures, colors and values. Many people also enjoy looking at such work in their homes and offices. It seems that artists who work in traditional ways will always find a large audience.

Many of today's artists enjoy working with new materials, processes and techniques. They like to experiment with new ideas, to challenge viewers to think in new ways. Their art will not look traditional and their visual statements will be different from those of the past.

Sculptor Doug Hyde communicates a strong cultural influence in Window Rock Woman. *It is a 73" (184 cm) high limestone sculpture. Courtesy Louis Newman Galleries, Beverly Hills.*

Clare Romano uses collagraph printmaking (printing from built-up surfaces) to communicate her feelings and impressions of the land. In Deep Canyon *she has cut a single plate into three segments, inked it with seven colors and made this print.*

Don Sevart forms glass tubes and fills them with gas to produce glowing works. Rocker *is of neon and is formed by a living line of lights.*

Eileen Senner combines many materials to create her experimental forms. Boat of Courage *is made of hardware cloth (heavy screen), sand, housepaint, celluclay and powdered pigment. The 51" (130 cm) form suggests the hull of a boat.*

Christo is well known for developing wrapped objects as art projects. In 1983, he ended three years of preparation by surrounding islands in Florida's Biscayne Bay with woven plastic material. Surrounded Islands *remained for public approval for several weeks, then was completely dismantled.*

Some of these nontraditional artists work with new concepts, experimental media or different techniques. Some will use sound, light or electricity. Others use computers and machinery instead of brushes and paint. These artists are excited by working with new and unconventional materials and tools. Some also enjoy using traditional materials in nontraditional ways.

People who enjoy stimulating artwork may purchase such pieces for their homes or offices. There are museums and galleries which specialize in handling the work of nontraditional, experimental or avant-garde artists.

Artists can find many ways to express themselves. There are unlimited combinations possible between the extremes of traditional and experimental art. Just as we all see things differently because of our different experiences and backgrounds, artists also work differently. This variety of expression has been called *pluralism*. Such pluralism can be seen in the works shown in this section of your book.

Gene Gill creates serigraphs (silk-screen prints) with many colored lines, often applied to several sheets of Plexiglas. His original technique produces exciting prints, such as Linear Polychroma, *a 24″ × 24″ (161 × 161 cm) work.*

Suggested Activities

1. Obtain copies of contemporary art magazines (*Art News, Art in America, Artforum, American Artist*) and cut out examples of traditional and nontraditional images. Arrange a bulletin board display or prepare a poster or notebook to show the *pluralism* of contemporary artistic expression.
2. Using traditional materials found in your art room (paper, paints, ink, pencils, scraps of wood, cloth) create some experimental artwork. Follow a model in this book or in a magazine.
3. If possible, visit local galleries or museums to acquaint yourself with the work of contemporary artists. Perhaps a class trip can be arranged.
4. Visit an artist in his or her studio or have an artist visit your classroom. They may be able to demonstrate their work for you. Listen to what is said and ask questions to help you understand why and how they work.

Understanding Art in Your World

Gregory Curci, painted aluminum, Peacock. 48 × 32 × 18" (122 × 81 × 46 cm). Courtesy David Bernstein Gallery.

6 The Elements and Principles of Design

The *elements of design* are the visual features of a work of art. They are the basic ingredients all artists use to create their work, and they are what we notice when we look at paintings, sculptures, buildings, crafts and commercial designs.

The *principles of design* are guidelines that artists and designers observe when they put the elements to work. These principles organize the parts of any work of art to make it most effective.

The elements and principles of design provide the structure for all kinds of artwork. In a given work, these qualities do not exist separately; they are combined to create unified products. However, each has distinct properties.

The Elements of Design

Line

If asked to describe line, you could say that there are straight lines as well as curved, diagonal and horizontal lines. You could also say that lines may be light, dark, of various colors, broken, fuzzy, hard, thick or thin.

Another quality of line is that it can provide direction. A line-like arrow is often posted to direct people to entrances, exits and elevators. Lines are painted on streets to indicate driving lanes.

The quality of line is affected by the materials used to produce it. Crayon will make different kinds of lines than ink. Chalk lines are different from those made with pencil.

Another characteristic of line is that it can have three dimensions: that is, it can have length, width and depth. Branches on a tree, a flagpole, wire, television antennas and the spokes of a bicycle wheel are all three-dimensional lines.

Then, too, there are implied lines. These are not actually lines as described above. They are line-like qualities such as those seen along the edges of buildings, boxes and the contours of countless objects. The line around a painted apple is an example of implied line. It is not really there in nature, but is needed to show an apple on paper. Think of other places where there are implied lines.

4-9

Cartoonists use line because it reproduces well in newspapers and magazines. Roger Armstrong uses pencil lines to sketch his Scamp characters, then inks the lines with pen and brush. Courtesy the artist and Walt Disney Productions.

In the glue print at right, the student artist put down the lines with white glue squeezed from a plastic bottle. When dry, the design was inked and printed. How would you describe these lines?

The lines in the student batik show great variety, from very thin to very bold. Some are outlines while others are the result of the batik process. Are the lines mechanical or organic?

Line is often a dominant feature in the work of artists and designers as they represent people, objects and nature.

Shape and Form

You will see shape and form wherever you are. The clouds in the sky are soft, fluffy, white forms. A sign on the side of a bus may be rectangular. A leaf has an irregular outline. The world in which you live is made up of shapes and forms that contrast in size, color and surface quality.

Shapes are flat and two-dimensional, and may be divided into two groups: *geometric* (square, rectangle, triangle, circle, oval) and *organic* (irregular in outline).

Forms are three-dimensional, and are also geometric (cube, pyramid, sphere, cylinder, cone) and organic (free-flowing masses).

The last birthday card you sent was probably rectangular. The cool, refreshing soda came in a can that was cylindrical.

Some shapes and forms are very large, such as the rectangular shape of a football field or the form of a huge mountain. Others are small as a piece of confetti or a small pebble.

Shapes and forms also differ in color and texture. They may be of bright or dull colors, may be rough or smooth, hard or soft, solid, hollow or have open spaces.

Visit a museum, art fair or local building, or look at art in this book. Notice how artists use shape and form. Try to describe some of the shapes and forms they use.

Shape and form are major features of both your natural and human-made environments.

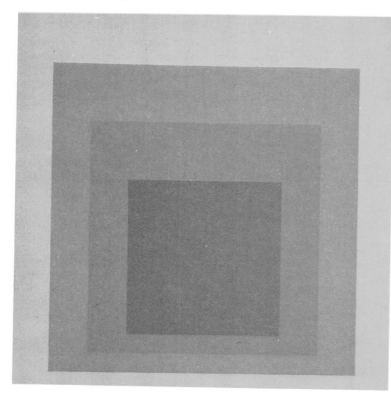

Joseph Albers emphasized geometric shapes in his oil painting. Homage to the Square: Glow, 1966. *Both color and shape are equally important elements in this two-dimensional work. (Hirshhorn Museum, Washington, D.C.) The student's starfish emphasizes three-dimensional, organic form. How many contrasts can you note between the two works?*

Andrew Wyeth's Christina's World, *1948 represents space and depth. How did the artist suggest space and depth on a two-dimensional picture plane? Courtesy The Museum of Modern Art, New York.*

Space

Each day you move through a variety of spaces, such as your room, classroom or library. As you walk out of your house, you enter a larger space—your neighborhood, which is part of even larger spaces (community, town or city). If you live in the country, the openness is emphasized by rolling hills or fields, to which you see no end. Even the earth moves on a rather regular course through an immense and endless space.

Designers of spaces must consider first how the space is to be used. For example, the automobile stylist must provide spaces for the engine, passengers, spare tire and luggage. To determine the space needed for an elevator, a designer must know how many people will ride it.

Architects work with spaces both in and around buildings. It is important to design structures that fit their environment. In a tall office building, the enclosed space is divided into smaller spaces, adapted to many uses. Architects usually plan building en-

trances to include open spaces, green areas and plazas with fountains or sculpture. This gives the spaces human quality and scale.

The element of space is also important to artists and designers. Painters, printmakers and graphic designers usually work within a flat, two-dimensional space, which is called the ***picture plane***. They often try to show three-dimensional space on two-dimensional surfaces. Finished designs and paintings show at least two other kinds of space: ***positive*** and ***negative***. For example, in a painting of a figure, the figure itself is the ***positive space***. The area around the figure is called the ***negative space***.

The three-dimensional work of sculptors occupies actual space. The sculpture and the space act on one another. It is important that the space around a piece of sculpture (negative space) complement the design.

Space, like line, shape and form, may be described as a major feature of your total environment, and may range in size from a tiny box to the entire universe.

The student who made this tissue collage used warm colors to communicate a hot desert feeling. The graphic designer of the NBC peacock used color to attract attention to the corporate logo.

Color, Value and Texture: Surface Qualities

Among the most important features of your world are its wide variety of colors, values and textures: green grass, blue sky, multicolored flowers, the brightness of daylight as reflected by different surfaces, the soft fur of a dog or cat. Everywhere you look you see colors, values and textures. Can you imagine a world without them? Discuss this idea.

Color, value and texture are surface qualities: that is, they are qualities that describe the outside surface of all natural and human-made things. You can see these qualities because of the light that various surfaces reflect. When you turn out the lights at night, all the colors, values and textures in your room seem to disappear. They are still there, but without light you cannot see them.

Color, value and texture give identity to things. The body of a new automobile may be described as blue (color), smooth and shiny (texture) and with light and dark tones (value). A rose in the sunlight may seem all red, but as you look closely, you will note many different tints and shades of red.

Color has three basic properties: *hue, value* and *chroma*. Hue is simply the name of a color; red, purple and yellow are hues. Value is the lightness and darkness of color. Red may be very light (pink), or very dark (maroon), or one of many tints or shades in between. Chroma is the intensity of color, ranging from brilliant and radiant to dull and grayed.

There are three basic colors, known as *primary colors*, that are used to produce all others: *red, yellow* and *blue*. Mixing two primary colors produces the *secondary colors: orange, green* and *purple*. Arranged in a circle (as on a color wheel), red is opposite green; blue across from orange; and yellow opposite purple. These opposing colors are called *complementary colors*. If you wish to change the intensity of a color (for example, to make it duller),

COLOR WHEEL

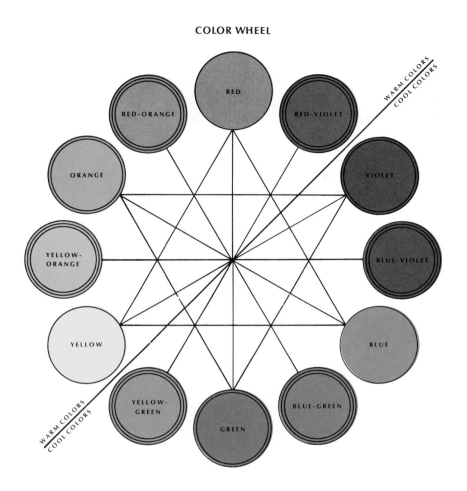

add a portion of its complement. Try it. (See the art activities at the end of this chapter.)

To explore the possibilities of value in color, select any of the primary colors. Add white to it. Does it get lighter? Add more white. How many different *tints* can you make? Use the same primary color, and add black. Note the change. How many *shades* of the color can you make?

These basic properties of color are important to artists and designers. Painters combine different colors, values and intensities to create realistic paintings, to show exciting relationships between abstract shapes and to vary moods. Graphic designers use color to communicate ideas and attract attention. Architects introduce color to provide contrast and emphasis. Craftspeople use color in weaving, jewelrymaking and ceramics for special appeal.

Texture, like color and value, is a visible surface quality. Unlike color and value, however, texture can be experienced through your sense of touch. You can understand texture by seeing and touching surfaces.

Words such as smooth, slick, silky, velvety, soft, prickly, rough and fluffy all describe different kinds of surfaces. Can you think of things that have surface qualities such as these?

You react to different textures in different ways. Some textures are smooth and pleasant and draw you to them, such as a soft chair or a fluffy pillow.

Other textures are scratchy and unpleasant. Can you think of some?

Artists, particularly sculptors and craftspeople, work on actual textures—surfaces that you can touch and understand by feeling. Painters may use such textures, but more often they create surfaces that only ***appear*** to be textured. Our eyes learn to comprehend actual textures, and this experience can be duplicated in two dimensions by skillful painters or printmakers.

Color, value and texture are found in many combinations and in contrasting situations. These ever-present art elements help you identify and describe the things around you.

The artist who designed these chairs was aware of the textural contrasts of the materials (hand rubbed woods and woven rope). Can your eyes "feel" the various textures? Moller chairs (Denmark) by Scan, Baltimore.

Painters often simulate textures in their work. Although this watercolor is on smooth paper, your eyes "see" the simulated textures of wood, stone, water, beach and trees. Watercolor by Gerald F. Brommer.

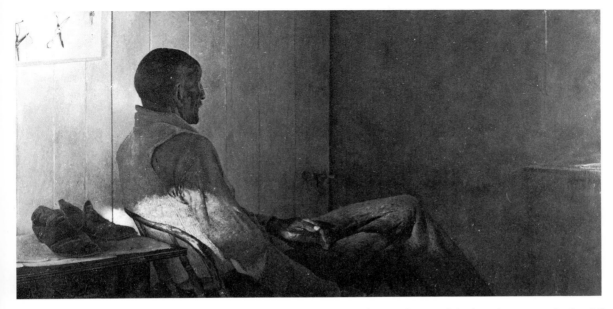

The Principles of Design

When we talk about the principles of design, we mean the way art elements are organized to produce various kinds of *balance, unity, contrast, emphasis, movement, rhythm and pattern*. These principles are always present in the work of artists and designers and are part of your natural environment.

Not everything you see is an example of good organization. This is particularly true in the human-made environment, where it often seems that no thought has been given to design. For example, think of roads and streets that are lined with a wild variety of billboards, restaurants and gasoline stations. Large and flashy signs compete to catch your attention. This environment is ugly and visually confusing.

Artists and designers use the principles of design to organize art elements and materials and to create appeal and interest.

Balance

There are three basic types of visual balance: *symmetrical*, *asymmetrical* and *radial*.

Symmetrical or *formal balance* is based on a work's vertical central line or axis. For example, in a

The papier-mâché piece is symmetrical, while the painting by Andrew Wyeth is asymmetrical. How did Wyeth use values and shapes to add a feeling of balance in The Gentleman? *Dallas Museum of Fine Arts, Texas.*

61

painting that is symmetrically balanced, everything to the right of center is nearly the same as everything to the left of center. Stand in front of a parked automobile. How is it an example of symmetrical balance? Look at a building. If the main entrance is directly in the center, balanced by windows equally spaced on either side, the building is symmetrically balanced. Symmetrical balance makes things look solid and uniform.

Asymmetrical or *informal balance* is the most common type of organization used by today's artists and designers. In an asymmetrically balanced work, art elements create a feeling of activity. In a painting, a large shape close to the left of center may be balanced by a smaller shape farther to the right. Asymmetrical balance creates movement and excitement. Look at newspaper and magazine ads, packages, labels and posters and determine the type of balance the artists used.

The third type of balance, *radial balance*, is based on the circle. The features of the design come from a central point. One of the most common examples is the wheel, because its spokes radiate from the center. Is there a church in your town that has a window based on radial balance? What things in nature might have radial balance?

Designs with radial balance are usually rather restful and quiet, and are also symmetrically balanced.

Unity

Unity is a sense of oneness, a feeling that everything works together to make a unified whole. Something that is unified projects a feeling of order and completeness.

Examples of unity and disunity are in every community. Is there a junkyard in your town? If so, visit it with a notebook or sketchbook. Note how the pieces of junk, tossed into piles or scattered about, seem unrelated. How does this contrast with a planned group of houses in your town? Or with a shopping area where buildings, trees, landscaping and streets have been carefully planned? In these, do you get the feeling that each part has been designed to relate to the others?

Artists and designers seek unity in their work by arranging shapes, colors, textures and content. Look at posters and paintings. If you feel that your eye moves directly and smoothly from one point to another, there is unity. Technique, media, style, composition and subject matter all help develop unity. Discuss how this may be so.

Contrast

How many contrasts do you see in the world around you? Think of the colors, textures and shapes in your home or school. There are light colors, dark colors; smooth surfaces, rough surfaces; the large spaces in a room and the small space in a desk drawer. There are contrasts in line from straight to curved, from thick to thin, from black on white to white on black. Contrasts add interest and excitement to your surroundings and to your art.

Artists and designers use contrast to create variety and excitement in their work. Study a painting or a

Clare Romano's collagraph, Red Canyon, *is printed in seven colors from a four-piece, segmented plate. Can you list the contrasts that the artist used in this work? How is unity achieved?*

How did puppet designer Roland Sylwester use contrast in each of these three puppets? Consider color, texture, form, fabrics and pattern.

piece of sculpture. How many ways has the artist used contrast? Consider contrasts of warm and cool colors; large and small shapes; textured and smooth areas; thin and thick lines; dark and light values. Look at buildings and their landscaping. Note the contrasts of materials. How does the architect use contrasts to add interest?

Even though all artists use contrast in their work, the finished products must still show some unity.

Emphasis

Graphic designers use contrasting sizes of lettering or type to create advertisements. These contrasts give emphasis to an important word or group of words. The painter, sculptor, stylist and craftsperson emphasize parts of their designs to attract attention. They direct your eye, in an orderly way, from one point to another. They want to give their work a center, an area of strongest interest. Often areas of great contrast (dark and light, for example) provide emphasis.

The term "emphasis" is also used to describe an idea that artists want to make clear in their work. For example, a painter might wish to emphasize movement, quiet, terror or beauty in a watercolor. He or she might place emphasis on abstract design or things that look realistic.

Look at a painting, a piece of sculpture and a newspaper advertisement. Determine the main emphasis in each. How has the artist or designer used color, value, texture, shape or line to provide emphasis?

The center of interest in Mary Cassatt's painting, Bathing the Young Heir, *is the baby's face. Why is the mother's face not the center of interest? How do the arms lead your eye to the central point? How does contrast help establish the area of greatest interest? Whitney Museum of American Art, New York.*

The emphasis in Betty Davenport Ford's Flying Gibbon *is on the stylization and form of the animal. Notice that all directional movement ends at the triangular face (center of interest).*

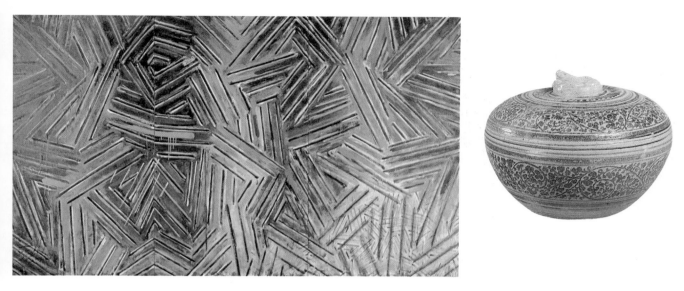

Jasper Johns used an irregular, repeated arrangement of lines and values for the patterned surface of Between the Clock and the Bed, *1983. The painting is done in encaustic (melted wax) and is 72" × 126" (182 × 321 cm), Leo Castelli Gallery, New York.*

A linear pattern and a vine-and-leaf pattern were combined by the Thai craftsperson who decorated this covered box in the fifteenth century. Los Angeles County Museum of Art.

Pattern

Pattern refers to actions of elements that happen again and again. We have patterns in our daily lives: waking, eating breakfast, getting ready for school. You do these things almost every day. Can you think of other patterns in your daily activity?

Everywhere you look you see lines, colors and values that are arranged to form patterns. Some patterns are formed by designers who repeat elements such as line, shape, color and texture. Look for patterns in fabrics, floor coverings, draperies and wallpaper. Pattern can be seen in buildings, wrapping paper and pottery. Pattern can be either two- or three-dimensional. How would ceramists use patterns in their clay work?

Architects and industrial designers often use patterns to provide interesting surfaces. Can you find these patterns?

Can you think of patterns found in nature? How do leaves, tree bark and pine cones use pattern? Which animals have patterns on their hides?

How have the architects used pattern to finish the outer surfaces of their buildings?

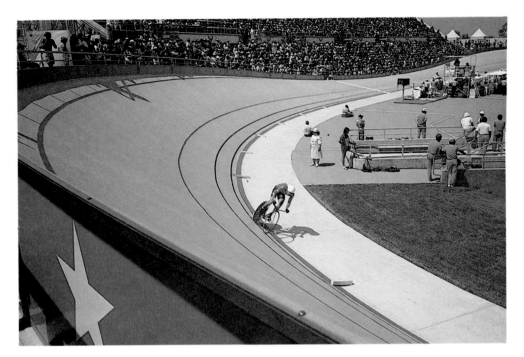

Notice the paths of movement created in this photograph by the long ripple of the orange stadium wall and the curved, radiating lines of the track. Can you feel the speed and movement of the cyclist? Marcel Routh, Velodrome, 1984 Olympics, 17 × 20" (43 × 51 cm).

Movement and Rhythm

Artists and designers often repeat shapes, figures or objects to create movement and rhythm. Rows and rows of windows and the use of contrasting materials (brick, concrete, glass) give rhythm to the surface of a building. The vertical (up and down) lines of high-rise buildings seem to move upward. Artists can make the movement in a work of art slow and steady or fast and exciting.

Painters use visual movement to lead us to a work's center of interest. They may use both dark and light shapes or lines to establish movement. Repeated shapes, lines, colors or objects give a painting visual rhythm.

Look for examples of movement and rhythm in your house or neighborhood. Try to look for movement and rhythm in paintings or sculpture.

Summary

Balance, unity, contrast, emphasis, movement, rhythm and pattern are principles of design. Artists and designers use them in a creative way to give their ideas life. As you learn about these principles, you will find that they help you appreciate and enjoy all forms of art more. Using the elements of art (line, shape, form, space, color, value and texture) will help you express yourself better when you create your own art.

Suggested Activities

1. On a large sheet of paper, see what kinds of lines you make with different media: crayon, pencil, chalk, brush and ink, pen and ink, markers.
2. Using soft wire, create a three-dimensional stick figure. Put your figure in a running pose.

3. How many shapes and forms can you see around you? Draw a few in your sketchbook or on a sheet of paper.

4. Make a rounded form from a lump of moist clay. Then change the form by pushing and pulling the clay. Create an imaginary animal form.

5. List five shapes and five forms. Then use adjectives to describe the size, texture, color and other unique qualities of each one.

6. Cut out five circles of different sizes from construction paper. Place them on paper of a contrasting color. Notice how some seem farther away than others. Overlap some, and notice the changes in their relationships to one another. Try different arrangements and discuss what happens.

7. Using tempera paints, mix red into yellow. What happens? Now mix blue into yellow; and then blue into red. Mixing two primary colors produces the secondary colors orange, green and purple. If you mix a secondary color with a primary color, you get an intermediate color such as yellow-orange.

8. Mix some green into red tempera paint. What happens? Add more green. Look at how the red changes as you add more green. If you keep adding green, you will end up with gray. Experiment with other complementary combinations (opposite colors on the color wheel).

9. Make a list of things that may be described as jagged, rough, granular, smooth, bristly, furry.

10. Place a piece of paper over a rough surface. Rub it with the side of a crayon to pick up the textures. Make a display of ten such rubbings.

11. Make a mask or butterfly design, emphasizing symmetrical balance. Use colored papers and paint.

12. Cut photographs from magazines and paste them on paper. Draw a line down the middle of each and decide if they are symmetrical or asymmetrical in balance. Try to find several examples of each type.

13. Create a painting, using one color and black and white. Such paintings are called ***monochromatic*** paintings. Note the unity created by your use of only one color.

14. Draw the outline of an object with pencil. Shade the inside of the object with vertical (up and down) lines. Does the surface show unity?

15. Take photographs of contrasts: rough and smooth, dark and light, soft and hard. Mount and display your pictures.

16. Cut five photographs from magazines and paste them on a large sheet of paper. Use a crayon to make a circle around the area that shows the most contrast.

17. Take a series of photographs of things in your environment. Each of your pictures should show one (or more) of the art elements.

18. Cut pictures of paintings or illustrations from magazines. Mount them on paper. With a crayon or marking pen, circle the center of interest in each. Then mark the light and dark value paths that lead your eyes to this center of interest.

19. Make a display of patterns found in nature and in human-made things. Cut pictures from magazine advertisements or take photographs of patterns you see.

20. Make a series of rubbings (with soft pencil on thin paper) of patterns. Find some natural patterns and some patterns that people have made. Display them together.

7 The History of Art

You do not exist in a vacuum. You have many contacts with people, books, movies, and music. These contacts inform and affect you. You have personal responses to your culture as you grow and change.

Culture has many definitions. In the arts, *culture* refers to human-made elements of life that give us beauty and enjoyment. Artists, musicians and writers always have given direction and flavor to our culture.

Your artistic culture has been influenced by Egyptians, Greeks, Romans; by Europeans, Asians, Africans, Eskimos, Indians, Mexicans. It has been influenced by people from ancient times, the Middle Ages and the Renaissance. Your culture has been influenced by many people and events around the world. To understand your artistic culture, look into history.

Ancient Times

Remember the last time you crossed a bridge? Saw a round arch? Looked at a stone column? Walked around a sculpture? Your enjoyment of them is your thanks to the ancients who first created them.

Do you like to put pictures on your walls? Ancient people also decorated their cave-homes with drawings of animals and people. In France, Spain and Africa, you can still see their decorations, even though many are thousands of years old.

The **culture of Egypt** was most important from about 3000 B.C. to 500 B.C. Egyptian artists worked on wall paintings, sculptures, huge buildings, temples and pyramids. These were for the rich and powerful rulers. Egyptians were very concerned with life after

The Parthenon (dedicated in 438 B.C.) is on top of the Acropolis of Athens. Other classic buildings are also located on the Acropolis.

Ancient Egyptian structures are usually very large. The Great Sphinx is 120' (36 m) high. The large pyramid of Cheops (at right) is 560' (176 m) high and 670' (276 m) long on each side of its base. Measure these distances out on your athletic field. Tombs were placed in and under such structures. The pyramid of Cheops was built in approximately 2530 B.C.

death. They filled the tombs of their leaders with artifacts such as art objects, statues and pictures of the animal-gods. These were for the dead to enjoy in their second life.

The development of countries in the Near East and the eastern Mediterranean Sea continued. There were many great cultural achievements in Babylon, Assyria, Persia, Crete, Mycenae and Greece. Although **Greek civilization** is recorded as early as 1100 B.C., its art became important after 500 B.C. Beautifully proportioned sculpture and architecture were the joy of Greek people during the Golden Age of Pericles, 480–404 B.C. At this time, the Acropolis in Athens was crowned with the Parthenon, still one of world's most beautiful buildings.

Greek architects introduced the carved column to history. They also created several different kinds of carved tops for these columns (Ionic, Doric, Corinthian). They built theaters and temples, many of which are still standing. They often decorated the floors of their homes and shops with mosaics of polished stones. Their sculpture—usually of male and female gods—influenced future generations of artists.

Roman art built on what the Greeks began. From 100 B.C. to 300 A.D., the Romans increased the size of their empire. Captured nations provided the work force to construct huge buildings. Roman architects used the arch in their aqueducts and bridges. They built domes and bridges of brick and concrete which they invented. Their buildings often were very large and held many people. Roman artists also designed mosaics of stone and glass to decorate their buildings. They used fresco paintings (paintings of colored plaster) for added interest. Of course, they continued sculpting, often copying the Greeks. The Romans built the Colosseum, the Pantheon, and many baths, basilicas, theaters and forums. All of these greatly influenced the work of later architects.

The Nike (Winged Victory) of Samothrace is 8' (2.5 m), and was carved from marble in about 200 B.C. Greek sculptors were master carvers of cloth and the human figure. They carved the wings from separate blocks and attached them to the body. Photograph courtesy French Government Tourist Office.

After twelve years of work, the Colosseum in Rome was finished in 82 A.D. It was 620' (190 m) long, held as many as 70,000 spectators and could be emptied in several minutes. Photograph courtesy Istituto Italiano di Cultura.

This Roman mosaic (second century) is made of tiny colored pieces of stone, about 150 in each square centimeter. The surface is polished to feel like glass. The entire work is 34" (85 cm) high. Capitoline Museum, Rome.

In Byzantine painting, stylization and symbolism were more important than realism. This thirteenth century Enthroned Madonna *was created with tempera paint on a 32" (80 cm) wooden panel. The background is gold. National Gallery of Art, Washington, D.C. (Gift of Mrs. Otto H. Kahn).*

The Middle Ages

The Roman Emperor Constantine became a follower of Christianity. He decided to move his capital to Byzantium (now Istanbul). A new era in art began. early Christians had decorated their tiny hidden chapels with primitive symbols. In 313 A.D., Christianity became a legal religion and churches were built. Religious decorations then appeared on walls and ceilings. The first churches were long, narrow meeting halls. They were copies of the Roman basilicas. The church designers used mosaics of Christian symbols and pictures from the Bible for decoration.

In **Byzantium**, however, a new style of building was designed with a huge dome over its center. The first great church, the Hagia Sophia (Holy Wisdom), has a dome that is 104 feet in diameter. It is supported by four huge groups of columns called *piers*. When it was built, it was the largest single room in the world. It is 141 feet high inside the dome. The inside of the building is shaped like a Greek cross, with four equal arms. It is completely covered with mosaics, made of brightly-colored glass and gold. This masterpiece became a model for hundreds of churches in Eastern Europe.

In Western Europe, the basilica shape was changed and cross arms (*transepts*) were added. This gave the appearance of a huge Latin cross. The main part of the church (the *nave*) became the long part of the cross. During the **Romanesque period** (approximately 800–1100 A.D.), the church was the main form of architecture. This is because it was also the town hall, the meeting place and the theater. The market was usually closeby. The buildings were constructed of stone. They had arch-shaped ceilings (called *barrel vaults*) and were heavy and gloomy. Typical churches had thick walls, small, round-arched windows and very little outside decoration. In Italy,

The interior of the Hagia Sophia in Istanbul is a huge open space. Its original colorful mosaics were covered with plaster when the Moslems conquered Constantinople.

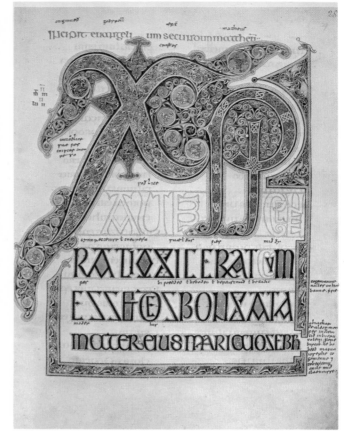

Medieval monks were excellent decorators of manuscripts. This multicolored page from the Lindisfarne Gospel Book *(698–721) is an example of their work. The delicate patterns and beautiful lettering are painted in egg tempera and gold on parchment. British Museum, London.*

the outsides of churches were covered with white and colored marble. The inside walls and ceilings were decorated with paintings and mosaics. A bell tower (*campanile*) was separate from the church building. One famous example of a bell tower is the Leaning Tower of Pisa.

In the **Gothic period** (about 1150–1400 A.D.), churches and buildings became increasingly larger, higher and wider—until one collapsed. Gothic architects learned from earlier buildings and added some new ideas: flying buttresses, decorative outsides,

pointed arches and various technical improvements. These enabled Gothic architects to construct huge buildings with large spaces inside for worship. Great stained glass windows were designed. Some of them were round (rose or wheel windows). Many of these marvelous structures are still in use in European cities: Notre Dame in Paris, Westminster Abbey in London and the cathedrals of Milan, Cologne, Florence and Chartres. Gothic public buildings that are still used include the guild halls of Brussels, the city halls of Munich and of Siena, Italy and the Doges Palace in

Notre Dame in Chartres (1194–1220) has both Romanesque (right) and Gothic spires. The inside of the stone cathedral, with its gorgeous Rose Windows, is considered one of the most beautiful of all Gothic churches. Photograph courtesy French Government Tourist Office.

Venice. See if you can find pictures of these buildings in an art book or encyclopedia.

Architecture was the *major* public art form during the Middle Ages. Other artists were busy decorating manuscripts, designing jewelry, painting murals (pictures on walls), making mosaics, building stained glass windows and sculpting decorations for the buildings.

The Renaissance

The **Renaissance** was a period (about 1400–1600 A.D.) of great artistic achievement in Europe, particularly in Italy. Painters and sculptors (also scientists) became very aware of the relationship between nature and humanity. They tried to imitate it. There was renewed interest in classic Greek and Roman art and studies. All of this interest in people, feelings and the environment followed the Middle Ages, when the church did not allow such thoughts. Renaissance means "rebirth" or "reawakening." Can you explain why such a title is given to this period?

Painting and sculpture became the major art forms of the Renaissance. What had been the main art form in the Middle Ages? Artists of the **early Renaissance** made small but important changes. They showed people as individuals, rather than as symbolic figures. This first step led to greater changes. Eventually, artists were able to create realistic paintings of people, cloth, plants, rocks and sky.

Great painting masters of this early Renaissance period in Italy included Giotto, Duccio, Masaccio, and Peiro della Francesca. Donatello was the main sculptor. Brunelleschi led the field of architecture. He invented perspective drawing (making things appear to be three-dimensional). The cities of Siena and Florence were the centers of the Italian Renaissance.

Many names of the **High Renaissance** might be familiar to you: Sandro Botticelli, Leonardo da Vinci, Raphael Sanzio, Michelangelo Buonarotti. All were giants in the world of art.

Leonardo was an outstanding designer, painter, inventor and scientist. He left us dozens of notebooks full of sketches, scientific notes and inventive drawings. Michelangelo, one of the world's greatest sculptors, painted one of the more important paintings in the world—the huge ceiling of the Sistine Chapel in Rome. He was also one of the architects of St. Peter's Church, also in Rome. All this was happening about the time Columbus was sailing to America.

Craftspeople were busy during the Middle Ages making items for both church and home. This chalice was crafted in 1140 for Abbot Suger of Saint-Denis. It is made of sardonyx, gold, silver gilt, gems and pearls. National Gallery of Art, Washington, D.C. (Widener Collection).

Early Italian Renaissance painters struggled with problems of perspective and reality. The Raising of Lazarus *is part of a large alterpiece by Duccio. It is one of the first paintings that shows individual faces instead of symbols. Kimbell Art Museum, Fort Worth.*

Raphael painted The Alba Madonna (1509) in a circle (tondo). The figures are arranged classically (in a triangle). They are set in a quiet Italian landscape. National Gallery of Art, Washington, D.C.

Renaissance artists in Northern Europe used a lot of detail in their paintings. Flemish artist Jan van Eyck placed his figures for The Annunciation in a Gothic cathedral instead of in a Biblical local. He used a 36" panel to tell his story. National Gallery of Art, Washington, D.C. (Mellon Collection).

Albrecht Dürer, a German artist, was both a painter and printmaker. Knight, Death and the Devil (1513), less than 10" (25 cm) high, shows Dürer's skill with engraving tools. It is on a copper plate. Note line detail. Los Angeles County Museum of Art (Graphic Arts Council Fund).

Michelangelo sculpted his Moses in 1515 from a single 8' (2.4 m) block of marble. The sculpture is now located in a small church, Pietro in Vincoli, in Rome.

Do you notice a relationship between events in art and in world exploration at this time?

In Venice (Northern Italy), Titian was producing portraits and other paintings. He used ideas from Greek and Roman mythology. Farther north, in Flanders (now Belgium), Jan van Eyck was painting detailed oil paintings that had religious themes. Later, Pieter Bruegel painted the people and objects around him, following Renaissance thought. In Germany, Albrecht Dürer worked with religious and nonreligious subjects, showing very small details. He also became the world's foremost printmaker. He worked in woodcut and etching techniques. Hans Holbein, a German, did portraits in England. Eventually he became court painter to King Henry VIII.

Hundreds of other painters, sculptors, architects and craftspeople were busy during the Renaissance.

Peter Paul Rubens of Flanders used swirls of movement and emphasized texture and light in his paintings. The Holy Family with the Dove (1610), 54" (140 cm) high, contains rich color and action. Los Angeles County Museum of Art (Colonel and Mrs. George J. Denis Fund).

This bronze sculpture of Louis XIV of France has many characteristics of Baroque Art: swirling cloth, exaggerated curls, extreme refinement and highly decorated clothing. It was done by one of Bernini's associates, while the Italian sculptor was working in France. National Gallery of Art, Washington, D.C. (Samuel H. Kress Collection).

The works of art range from great wall murals created in Italy to tiny easel paintings created in Flanders; from the giant sculptures of Michelangelo to the detailed etchings of Dürer; and from the religious art of the Middle Ages to the artistic freedom of the Late Renaissance. It was a period of many great awakenings.

Baroque and Rococo

Renaissance artists found ways to give a natural appearance to their subjects. Artists of the 1600s were often influenced by the rapid change in religion, politics and trade. Their art reflected the dynamic confusion, unrest and energy of their times.

In this period, works of art became larger and technically complicated. Perspectives were distorted. Artists showed extremes of movement, excitement, light and shadow. The cool restraint of the Renaissance changed into the dynamic activity of the **Baroque**. New styles of operas and symphonies were composed in Italy. In Germany, Johann Sebastian Bach created complicated new musical patterns.

Architecture became important again. The dark, mysterious interiors of the Gothic cathedrals gave way to the bright, shiny, gold-colored swirls of the Baroque. The master architect and sculptor of the time was Lorenzo Bernini of Italy, who designed the huge, curved series of columns in front of St. Peter's Church. He sculpted fantastic, swirling figures and filled Rome with gloriously active fountains.

Caravaggio, in Italy, painted realistic people. He used light and dark shadow to express his feelings. Two great Spanish painters were Diego Velázquez, a native, and El Greco, a Greek who lived in Spain.

Northern Europe also produced great painters. In Flanders, Peter Paul Rubens's work showed Baroque largeness and swirling movement. Anthony van Dyck, from Flanders, became court portrait painter to

El Greco's painting St. Martin and the Beggar *swirls with flickering light and movement. Notice that all shapes and lines direct your eye to the head of St. Martin. He is giving his cloak to the beggar. National Gallery of Art, Washington, D.C. (Widener Collection).*

Rembrandt used deep shadows and bright highlights to bring life to his paintings. The Night Watch is a group portrait of a Dutch shooting company, with the commanders in the foreground. The large painting is more than 14' (4.3 m) wide. It is in the Rijksmuseum, Amsterdam.

Charles I of England. In Holland, Frans Hals portrayed smiling townspeople. Jan Vermeer showed the bright interiors of Dutch houses.

One Dutch master painter rose above other Baroque artists. Rembrandt van Rijn became one of the world's great artists. He painted and etched Biblical subjects, portraits and landscapes. He used shadow and controlled light to express deep feeling. His *Night Watch* and *Syndics of the Cloth Guild* are

Jean Baptiste Chardin painted The Attentive Nurse *(1738). He shows that ordinary people doing ordinary work are an important part of society. How did he show this? National Gallery of Art, Washington, D.C. (Samuel H. Kress Collection).*

very large and show many people. They also show careful control of light and shadow.

In France, the Baroque period was followed in the 1700s by the **Rococo style**, which was playful and aristocratic. Antoine Watteau, François Boucher and Jean Fragonard painted for the wealthy aristocracy. Jean Baptiste Chardin created pictures of everyday people and things. His work, aimed at common people, spread early seeds of democracy.

In Spain, Francisco Goya produced masterful paintings and etchings. His work expressed his nationalistic feelings. His *Executions of the Third of May* is a powerful statement about people's cruelty to others.

Some important English painters include Joshua Reynolds, Thomas Gainsborough and William Ho-

garth. They produced hundreds of portraits of the country's aristocracy. Hogarth also used his art to criticize immorality in the upper classes. At the same time, hundreds of other artists were depicting the events, people and thoughts of the day.

The Nineteenth Century

If you had been an art student in 1850, you would have had to decide what style of art to follow, from among several styles of art. In what way is this different from the Renaissance?

Classical architecture was revived with structures such as the Arch of Triumph in Paris. This structure imitates similar arches that Roman emperors built to honor themselves. Designed by J. F. Chalgrin in the 1800s, the Arch of Triumph was built by Napoleon to honor his army. Photograph courtesy of Trans World Airlines.

Jacques-Louis David's Oath of the Horatii *(1785) is based on an ancient Greek story. It shows the family united for a common cause. The Louvre, Paris.*

You might have chosen the style of Frenchmen Jacques Louis David and Jean Dominique Ingres. They developed the **Neoclassic style**—imitating and building on the features of ancient Greek and Roman art. Artists of the Neoclassic style used classical poses, dress, furniture and techniques. Architects used the Parthenon in Athens as their example when designing buildings. Neoclassical architecture has columns and classical proportions. If you were a student of drawing you would have studied and drawn plaster models of Greek sculpture.

Many artists (and you might have been among them) couldn't accept the rigid rules of the Neoclassical style. To them, art was an expression of feelings, not a set of art laws. Led by French painter Theodore Géricault and Eugène Delacroix, such people began the new style of **Romanticism**. Instead of creating artwork about ancient Greek life, they showed the Middle Ages (crusades, knights in armor, and life in Arab lands). Their architects returned to the Gothic style. Emphasis was on sharing the *feelings and emotions* of adventures, both past and present.

Romantic painters in England stressed the adventure in nature rather than in history. John Constable painted English skies and landscapes. William Turner, after first producing realistic paintings, created impressionistic works of sunsets, storms, fog, fire and light.

In America, a group of painters formed, called the Hudson River School. They repeated the landscape work of England and France, but used American subject matter. Several independent American painters were working, too. Among them was John James Audubon. He painted American birds and animals so that the English could see our wildlife.

If you did not like the rules of the Neoclassic artists nor the adventure of the Romantics, you could be a **Realist**. In France, several artists chose to show nature and people just the way they saw them, without emotion. Camille Corot, Jean François Millet and Gustave Courbet became masters at this. They painted nature, showing real colors, textures and scenes.

In America, two men carried on the work of the Realists, Winslow Homer and Thomas Eakins. They

Eugène Delacroix led the opposition of Romantic artists to classicism. His Abduction of Rebecca *(1846) shows an event from the romantic adventure written by Sir Walter Scott. Collection of The Metropolitan Museum of Art, New York (Wolfe Fund).*

American realist painter Winslow Homer loved to paint the sea outside his home on the Maine coast. Breezing Up *is an oil painting, dated 1876. Collection of The National Gallery of Art, Washington, D.C. (Gift of the W. L. and May T. Mellon Foundation).*

Mary Cassatt was one of several Americans who worked in the Impressionist style. Sleepy Baby *is an example of her mother and child themes. It is done in pastel. Though it appears casual, the movement and values are carefully composed. They lead to the center of interest. Collection of the Dallas Museum of Fine Arts (Munger Fund Purchase).*

produced excellent landscapes and portraits. Two other famous American artists, James McNeill Whistler and John Singer Sargent, did most of their work in France and England. William Harnett painted still lifes. Charles Russell and Frederic Remington painted and sculpted the wild West. They showed us soldiers, Indians, cowboys, bucking broncos and gunfights.

Impressionism and Post-impressionism

Stand in a sunny spot outdoors and close your eyes. Now open them quickly for a split second and close them again. What did you see? What colors do you remember? What shapes can you recall? Did you notice any details? Did you see any fine lines or individual leaves or flowers?

Near the end of the nineteenth century (approximately 1875) there were several painters who followed the Realist technique and painted outdoors. But the more they worked in the sunlight, the more they became interested in the colors and values in nature, rather than in lines, shapes and forms. They painted the light and colors of sunshine on grass, water and trees. They showed us the split-second impressions that they had, as if their paintings were pictures from the newly-invented camera. Frenchmen Edouard Manet, Claude Monet, Auguste Renoir, Edgar Degas and an American, Mary Cassatt, used new painting techniques to create impressions of people and landscapes.

Impressionism often uses light colors, very little black paint, summertime subject-matter and no detail. In Impressionism, brush strokes are meant to be seen. This was a completely new approach to painting, and, of course, many people (even other artists) did not like what the Impressionists were doing.

The greatest sculptor at this time was Auguste Rodin, who also experimented with new techniques

August Rodin made his bronze sculptures express the feelings of his subjects. The Burghers of Calais *shows us the six city officials who offered their lives to the enemy to save their city. Can you feel the tension as they make their commitment? Rodin Museum, Paris.*

for forming clay and casting bronze. Rodin created a *feeling* of his subject rather than an exact likeness. Many people did not like this idea. They wanted sculptures to look exactly like real people.

Later in the nineteenth century, several artists were not satisfied with the seemingly incomplete work of the Impressionists. They wanted to make more solidly designed paintings. Paul Cézanne, one of these **Post-impressionist** painters, was a careful designer of pictures. He arranged his subjects deliberately. He often worked from still-lifes or landscape scenes. He always rearranged his material. He felt it was more important to make the arrangement of the painting just right than to try to imitate the light and color of

Claude Monet observed nature and light with great care. He often painted the same subject at different times of the day. Rouen Cathedral, West Façade, Sunlight *is one of more than fifty paintings he did of the same subject. Squint your eyes a bit to see the forms. The National Gallery of Art, Washington, D.C. (Chester Dale Collection).*

Vincent van Gogh painted The Starry Night *to show that the universe is turbulent, even on a seemingly quiet night. He painted his feelings about people and places. He was an Expressionist painter. He was also one of the Post-impressionist artists. Collection of The Museum of Modern Art, New York (Lillie P. Bliss Bequest).*

nature. Of course, many people disliked this idea. Yet Paul Cézanne had a tremendous influence on twentieth century art.

Another Postimpressionist painter, Vincent van Gogh, communicated his very strong feelings. Paul Gauguin, who spent many years in Tahiti, painted an ideal civilization. Henri de Toulouse-Lautrec used the dance halls and cabarets of Paris as his subjects.

The work of the Impressionists and Postimpressionists allowed artists to express personal feelings in their own work. They were considered rebels in the nineteenth century, but they laid the foundation for today's personal experimentation and expression in art.

The Twentieth Century

Moving into twentieth century art is like flinging open a dozen doors at the same time. Everywhere you look, there is another door and another path to follow. But it all began with Cézanne's idea that the artist should be concerned with his artwork, not with imitating nature. The camera can produce likenesses, but the artist can produce art—his own personal arrangement and expression.

Several major doors were opened by Pablo Picasso, a Spaniard who spent most of his life in France. He and his friend, George Braque, began and developed a new style, **Cubism** (about 1907). Cubism takes apart the subject matter and reassembles it according to the artist's own design. Some kinds of Cubist painting allow you to see several views of the subject (a vase, for example) at the same time. These artists even began using *collage* (a painting which included pasted paper) in their work.

Abstract art (about 1910) began by showing nature as basic shapes and colors, often leaving out detail and shading. It developed to include paintings of flat, rich, colored shapes. Leading abstract artists

In this painting, Pablo Picasso has broken the three figures and put them together again in a different way. Three Musicians *has rich varieties of pattern, shape and color. It is large, 80" × 74" (203 × 188 cm). Look carefully to find several surprise shapes. The Philadelphia Museum of Art (A. E. Gallatin Collection).*

Wassily Kandinsky made non-objective paintings. The only subject matter in Improvisation No. 24 *(1912) is color, line, shape and movement. The Norton Simon Foundation, Los Angeles.*

Henri Matisse cut shapes from painted paper and glued them to create this collage. Some lines were painted on, but most of Madame de Pompadour *is brightly painted shapes. Los Angeles County Museum of Art (Gift of Mr. and Mrs. Sidney Brody).*

were Wassily Kandinsky, Picasso, Piet Mondrian and Stuart Davis. They created paintings of color and shape. Often you could not identify the subject. Such works are called **Nonobjective art**. How does this follow Cézanne's thinking about art and painting?

Several artists wished to express more feeling, rather than work in a cold and mathematical way. Edvard Munch, Georges Rouault, Picasso and Marc Chagall were such artists. They were called **Expressionists**, using color, form, line, value and texture in personal ways to reveal deep emotions about their lives and their world.

Other artists, including Henri Matisse, André Derain and Raoul Dufy, used *color* to express their ideas. They painted subjects that looked real. But

Georges Rouault shows deep feelings in his paintings, as in The Old King *(1937). Such emotional artists are called Expressionists. Museum of Art, Carnegie Institute, Pittsburgh.*

Naum Gabo used molded plastic and plastic threads to make this sculpture, Linear Construction. *How is this work different from Michelangelo's sculptures? Tate Gallery, London.*

they used wild, bright, pure color, often right from the tubes. This produced such vivid paintings that people called them wild beasts, or, in French, "les Fauves." Their art was called **Fauvism**.

During World War I, art came to a standstill. Afterward there were new materials (such as plastics) and a newfound freedom generally. This led to a style of sculpture called **Constructivism**. The old approaches, carving and casting, were no longer used to form sculpture. The Bauhaus (a German art school) became constructivism's center with Kurt Schwitters and Naum Gabo as leaders.

Salvadore Dali's The Sacrament of the Last Supper *appears realistic. But a closer look reveals a transparent body, a symbolic partial body and unnatural lighting. Such surrealism often makes use of complex detail and careful craftsmanship. The National Gallery of Art, Washington, D.C. (Chester Dale Collection).*

Willem de Kooning's Easter Monday *is a large abstract Expressionist work. It is 96" × 74" (244 × 188 cm). It stirs with color and action. Using oil and newspaper transfer, the artist has shown action and feeling. He did not use ordinary, easy to identify subject matter. Instead, action and color are his non-objective subjects. The Metropolitan Museum of Art (Rogers Fund), with permission of the artist.*

Several artists used a very personal, almost dream-like method. As it reached beyond the real world it was called **Surrealism**. In the surrealists' world, the objects seemed real enough, but the painting produced an unreal feeling. Salvador Dali, Yves Tanguy, Joan Miró and Paul Klée worked in this world, although other artists joined them from time to time.

Following World War II, a new method of painting developed in the United States. This style swept around the world. This freewheeling style allowed personal expression through color and brushwork, but in a nonobjective way. This style was called **Abstract Expressionism** (or Action Painting). It was advanced by Jackson Pollock, Lee Krasner, Hans Hofmann, Grace Hartigan, Willem de Kooning, Joan Mitchell, and Franz Kline. These artists didn't all work in the same ways. They developed their own ways of

Frank Stella's work was not bound by the traditional rectangular shapes. In Protractor Variation *(1969) he used geometric shapes and hard edges to create the 120″ × 240″ (305 × 610 cm) work. Los Angeles County Museum of Art.*

using color, brushwork, drips, slashes, swirls, textures and surfaces. Because the public was used to seeing trees, vases and people in paintings, many people found it hard to accept the new expressive art forms.

Contemporary Art

What is happening in art today? If there were a dozen doors to open in 1900, there are several hundred today. Artists have been freed from styles. Now artists can express their feelings in any way. New media, such as acrylic paints, also have opened new doors in art styles. Some of these are not always understood by observers, but the artists are still trying to communicate in new ways. All methods are acceptable today, but there are several major trends.

Hard Edge Painting is a relative of the first Abstract work. It has been refined to pure shape and color. Sometimes real objects or landscape shapes are used, but more often the work is nonobjective. Victor Vasarély, Josef Albers, Ellsworth Kelly, Max Bill and Helen Lundeberg are among the leaders in this style. This form has been called **Cool Art** because it lacks emotional emphasis.

As Abstract Expressionism slowly lost its intensity, a new style emerged from it. This style combined abstract areas of rich color with startlingly real images of rubber tires, radio parts or other found objects. Often actual items were attached to paintings, creating collages. Robert Rauschenberg and Jasper Johns produced such **Combine-Paintings**.

This leads directly into **Pop Art**, a style which uses subject matter and feeling of the "popular culture" of everyday, usable things. Pop Art glorifies hamburgers, soup cans, advertisements, comic strips, package labels, by showing them in giant sculptures

Here black vinyl imitates the hard, shiny covering of an electric fan in Claes Oldenburg's Giant Soft Fan. *It is 10' (3 m) high, soft and filled with foam rubber. Collection of The Museum of Modern Art, New York (The Sidney and Harriet Janis Collection).*

Judy Chicago used an airbrush (a small spray gun) to paint Virginia Woolf, *a 5' × 5' (1.5 × 1.5 m) acrylic work (above, right). Woolf is one in a series of three works in Chicago's* Reincarnation Triptych. *The series expresses the characteristics of three women whose lives influenced the artist.*

or paintings. It is fun, but it also makes a social comment about how much of everything we have today. Roy Lichtenstein, James Rosenquist, Claes Oldenberg and Andy Warhol lead in this style but there are many others who use it.

New materials, or new ways of using old materials, lead to another area of art today: contemporary sculpture. Neon tubing, plate glass, television sets, electronics, sound, strobe lights, laser beams, hydraulic mechanism, Plexiglas, plastics and holograms are all part of the contemporary sculptor's materials. What differences can you note from the days of Michelangelo?

Jasper Johns constructed this combine painting. He used encaustic (melted wax colors) and collage, together with actual objects. In the Studio *is 72" × 48" × 4" (182 × 122 × 10 cm). Courtesy Leo Castelli Gallery, New York.*

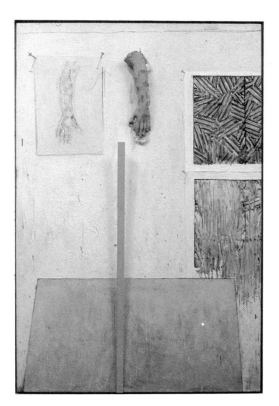

93

Louise Nevelson collected a fantastic array of wood pieces to produce Sky Cathedral. *The wood construction is over 11' (3.4 m) high, painted black. The Museum of Modern Art, New York (Gift of Mr. and Mrs. Ben Mildwoff).*

Suggested Activities

1. After studying this section on art history, it would be helpful to visit an art museum. Arrange to have a lecturer or your teacher discuss several paintings in the museum.

2. Collect art prints made available by your art teacher or librarian, or from art magazines. Arrange a display or make a scrapbook. Organize your examples chronologically. Each class member might work on a different time period. Select art that comes from Europe, America, Asia, India or Africa. How else might you organize a presentation?

3. Analyze one example of artwork according to the elements and principles of design (discussed on pages 54–67). Prepare a written or oral report, using prints or slides as examples.

4. Select an artist already discussed. Read about him or her in art history books, art dictionaries, encyclopedias or in art magazines. Prepare a written or oral report for your classmates.

5. Using tempera or watercolors, try to paint in the style of one of the artists discussed in this section of the book. Take special note of color, line, shape and texture.

Many cultural influences have touched your life. Some are shown in the chart. See if you can match the names with the pictures.

Siva, The Lord of Dance, *from India tenth century, bronze. The Los Angeles County Museum of Art (anonymous gift).*

Woman Dancer, *Torii Kiyonobu I, Japan, about 1708, woodcut. The Metropolitan Museum of Art (Harris Brisbane Dick Fund).*

Totem Fragment, *Northwest American Indian wood carving, painted. Whatcom Museum of History and Art, Bellingham, Washington (Gerber Collection).*

Weeping Woman with Handkerchief, *Pablo Picasso, oil on canvas, 1937. The Los Angeles County Museum of Art (Gift of Mr. and Mrs. Thomas Mitchell).*

Head Mask, *Bauli, Africa, carved and hollowed wood. Collection of Mr. and Mrs. Joseph Gatto, Los Angeles.*

Winged Genius, *from Assyria, ninth century B.C., gypseous alabaster, 93" (236 cm) high. The Los Angeles County Museum of Art (Donated by Anna Bing Arnold).*

Buddha Enthroned *from Cambodia (Khmer Empire), tenth century, bronze. Kimbell Art Museum, Fort Worth.*

Egyptian Relief Carving, *from Egypt, about 1500 B.C., tomb carving, now in the Louvre, Paris. Photograph courtesy of Air France.*

Form, *by Max Bill of Switzerland, granite, twentieth century. Photographed at the Los Angeles County Museum of Art.*

Bust of St. John the Baptist, *Rembrandt, oil on panel, 1632. The Los Angeles County Museum of Art (William Randolph Hearst Collection).*

Man Pointing, *Alberto Giacometti, 1947, bronze, 70" (178 cm) high. The Museum of Modern Art, New York (Gift of Mrs. John D. Rockefeller).*

8 Influences in Your Contemporary Culture

European culture was the primary influence for most of America's art and culture. From there it can be traced back through history to Greece and Rome. But African, Asian, Mexican and Native American ethnic influences have also shaped our contemporary art and culture.

In addition, machines and computers have influenced our culture. So have the furniture designs of Italy and the Scandinavian countries; and the automotive designs from Europe and Japan. Women have become increasingly important in determining the direction of American art and design. Wars, fads, international communication, increased mobility, space exploration, television and contemporary life-styles all, in some way, influence American art and culture.

Some influences are direct and others are indirect. Some effect us all. Others touch only some of us. But we are all influenced by people and ideas that come from all over the world. Fashion news in Paris is transmitted immediately to New York, Dallas and Atlanta. People in Los Angeles, Omaha and Chicago know immediately of Japanese automotive design changes. Television, magazines and newspapers provide a constant source of information to all Americans.

As people of our world are brought closer by increased travel and more sophisticated communications, these influences will become even stronger.

This T'ang Dynasty horse (800 A.D.) shows the great skill of Chinese ceramic artists. Three glaze colors were used on this 29" (74 cm) high horse. Collection, The Los Angeles County Museum of Art (Gift of Mr. and Mrs. Felix Guggenheim).

Dong Kingman bears witness to his Chinese heritage in *Wintertime: Great Wall, a 22" × 30" (56 × 76 cm) water-color. He combined elements from several places in China to compose this fascinating work.*

Susuki Harunobu created this color woodcut, Drying Clothes, *in 1767. Such prints, with strong line accents, made a great impression on European artists of the 19th century. Collection of the Philadelphia Museum of Art.*

Asian Influences

The cultures of India and China are more than 4000 years old. They have directly influenced the art, religion and daily life of all Asian peoples.

Chinese ceramics were very important, as were paintings, calligraphy, textiles, bronze sculptures and banners. The explorer Marco Polo returned to Europe with many examples of Chinese art. These influenced the art of his time, and of ours.

Many Japanese artists specialized in making wood-cuts. The colorful prints of Harunobu, Hiroshige, Hokusai and others influenced nineteenth-century European artists, especially the French Impressionists. And French Impressionism directly influenced the art and taste of nineteenth and twentieth century Americans.

Flat colors, decorative designs, thoughtful simplicity and Oriental perspective became important influences on American architects, landscape designers, painters, ceramists, printmakers and sculptors. Important contemporary Oriental-American artists include: I. M. Pei (architect, see chapter 4), Dong Kingman (painter), Isamu Noguchi (sculptor, see chapter 12), Tyrus Wong (designer) and Patrick Nagatani (photographer).

American culture reflects Oriental influence both *directly* and *indirectly* . Can you explain how this may be?

Black African Influences

Black African culture developed from a variety of individual societies, some of which are more than 6000 years old.

The farmers and hunters of southern Africa needed ceramic pots, decorated tools and carved statues of gods. All of these made life easier, more secure and more meaningful. The more complicated societies of central and western Africa (Ashanti, Benin and Mali, for example) developed sculpture, fabric design, ceramics, painting and bronze casting. Their art objects reflected beliefs in magic, a reverence for ancestors and respect for tribal leaders.

Long ago, African artists worked with abstract forms. They created idealized sculpture that were *concepts* of people, animals and gods. These sculptures were not realistic likenesses. This *conceptualized* approach to art had a great influence on European artists of the early twentieth century. Through them it influences us.

Pablo Picasso and Amedeo Modigliani (among others) studied African masks. The styles, designs, and conceptualized features of these masks changed these artists' ways of working and thinking. Because of this African influence, Picasso started the *cubist* style. It has influenced all of contemporary art.

Black American artists have used their art to express their historical concerns, frustrations and desires. Such artists include Romare Bearden (painter, collagist), Charles White (draftsman), Elizabeth Catlett (sculptor, printmaker), Sargent Johnson (sculptor), Faith Ringgold (painter), and Barkley L. Hendricks (painter).

Skilled in the casting of bronze, a late sixteenth century artist of Benin City, Nigeria, sculpted the 24" (62 cm) flutist. The surface is richly decorated and detailed. The figure is a concept, not a likeness. British Museum, London.

Ink has been applied with various tools to produce a dramatic textural surface in Charles White's 51" (130 cm) high Seed of Love. A skilled draftsman, the artist expresses the feelings and frustrations of his Black contemporaries. The Los Angeles County Museum of Art (Museum Purchase Fund).

Romare Bearden's The Dove is an example of his expert use of collage. He makes strong statements about his cultural heritage and the situation of Black Americans. Courtesy of the artist.

Mexican Influences

The Mayan, Toltec, Aztec and Mixtec cultures of Mexico became highly developed during the years 600–1521 A.D.. But even the more ancient cultures produced distinctive art and architecture. The simplified forms were mostly related to religion, funeral practices and the adornment of nobility. Huge pyramids and temples were built. Artists carved stones and made gold and jade into fine jewelry. They painted murals on walls and created drawings to decorate books.

When Europeans arrived in Mexico, they disrupted everything, including art. Artwork was destroyed and an important culture all but disappeared. Spanish architecture and art were combined with native styles. This produced a new kind of art that has greatly influenced art and especially architecture in America.

This stylized figure, made before Columbus arrived in America, is painted terra cotta. It was found in the ruins of Teotihuacan, near Mexico City. National Museum of Anthropology, Mexico City.

American architecture, especially in areas that border Mexico, has been greatly influenced by Mexican styles. Mission churches, such as San Xavier del Bac, south of Tucson, were built by Indians and directed by Spanish padres. These buildings still influence the style of many of today's structures.

Diego Rivera was Mexico's great muralist. He also produced easel paintings, such as Liberation of the Peon, *1931. Social themes are seen often in his works. Collection of the Philadelphia Museum of Art.*

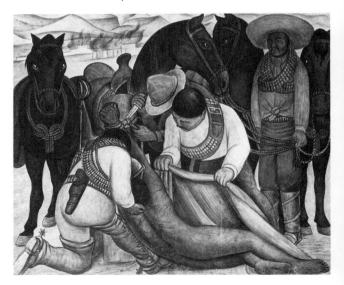

This Western Apache storage jar is 36" (91 cm) high. It is a fine example of basketry. Beautiful balance and sensitive decoration characterize this work. The Texas Memorial Museum, Austin.

Kevin Red Star produces portrait studies of Indians. He uses a modern approach that makes his work unique. Courtesy Treasure State Gallery, Great Falls, Montana.

Following the revolution of 1910–1920, Mexican artists such as Diego Rivera, Jose Clemente Orozco and David Alfaro Siqueiros produced huge murals. These illustrated social problems and concerns. The murals directly influenced painters in the United States. In fact, during the Depression, the U. S. government commissioned many murals for public buildings. Several were done by Mexico's great painters.

Strong national feeling, simplicity of forms and treatment of social conditions strongly influence Mexican art today. Many Mexican-Americans are active in our art world, including painters Michael Ponce de Leon, Porfirio Salinas, Glynn Gomez, Eugenio Quesada, Consuelo González Amézcua and Peter Rodriquez.

The parts of our country that border Mexico have been most strongly influenced by Mexican culture. The street paintings we have today are a direct inheritance from the Mexican muralists.

American Indian Influences

Years before Columbus landed in this hemisphere, North American Indians were creating works of art. In the Southwest, Native Americans made Kachina dolls, pottery, weavings, jewelry, sand painting and baskets. Northwest coast Indians created masks, baskets and carved wooden totems. Eastcoast Indians made porcupine-quill artwork, beadwork, wampum, leather goods and woodwork. Natives of our Great Plains painted hides, carved and painted tools and weapons and created baskets and leatherwork.

Now these artworks can be found in museums. American Indian art is as varied as the locations in which it was created. Some forms cannot be found anywhere else in the world.

Many Indian cultures were all but destroyed by the westward movement of settlers from Europe. Therefore, today's revival and production of Indian crafts is

American Indian artist Fritz Scholder considers his next step in painting Television Indian. *His painting process was taped in his Arizona studio for public television.*

very important to Native Americans and to our national cultural heritage.

Recently, some Indian artists have begun painting and sculpting in contemporary ways. Artists include Kevin Red Star (painter), Fritz Scholder (painter), Pablita Velarde (painter), Veloy Vigil (painter, printmaker) and Doug Hyde (sculptor). Their subject matter is influenced by themes such as love of nature, strength of character, conservation of natural resources, and the conditions of the entire Indian culture. Still these artists are communicating in the language of today's art.

Traditional Indian crafts and jewelry continue to be much admired. Beautiful black-on-black pottery by Maria and Julian Martinez is known worldwide. Potters such as Virginia Ebelacker, Lucy Lewis and Joseph Lonewolf are influenced by traditional designs and techniques.

The Influence of Women

History suggests that the vast majority of important American artists have been men. The last half of the twentieth century has seen an increasing number of influential women artists. Since at least the Renaissance, there have been women with active art careers, but their numbers appear to have been few. Often these women were the talented wives or daughters of well-known artists whose work and fame overshadowed that of skilled, artistic women.

With our culture's improvement in the status of women, there has been a change in the status of women artists. Women artists are rightfully receiving national and international acclaim. Museums and galleries are featuring their work with increasing regularity. Look through some current art magazines (***American Artist, Art News, Art in America***) and notice the number of articles and gallery advertisements that feature women artists.

Many women have worked hard to become outstanding artists, encountering tough competition for recognition. Prominent among them are Louise Nevelson (sculptor, see chapter 12), June Wayne (printmaker), Georgia O'Keeffe (painter), Lee Krasner (collagist, painter), Audrey Flack (painter), Marisol (sculptor), Helen Frankenthaler (painter) and Colleen Browning (painter). All are known for their personal styles and unique contributions to American art.

Increasing numbers of young women have become important members of contemporary art movements, including Judy Chicago (painter, sculptor), Bridget Riley (op art painter), Faith Ringgold (soft sculpture, mixed media), Rosemary Castoro (conceptual work, sculptor) and Janet Fish (painter). Their work is in the forefront of contemporary art. It will help determine the direction and foundation of twenty-first century art.

Georgia O'Keeffe painted From the Plains I. *It is an interpretation of spaces in western America. Large, simple forms are characteristic of her work. This oil painting is 48″ × 48″ (122 × 122 cm). McNay Art Institute, San Antonio.*

Judy Chicago has developed a unique way of making art. This embroidered work is 45″ × 27″ (114 × 69 cm), designed by the artist and fabricated by Catherine Russo. It is only one of many such panels which were done in various fabrics and completed by craftspeople all over the country. The assembled piece is called The Birth Project. *Its subject is women and the birth experience.*

Audrey Flack's A Pear to Heade and Heal *is realistically painted, but there are parts that trick our eyes. The acrylic work is 38" × 56" (97 × 142 cm). Courtesy Louis K. Meisel Gallery, New York.*

Other Influences on Our Culture

We are surrounded by products of the world's artists and designers. We have looked at some effects of ethnic and political influences. There are other influences as well.

Cameras have shown us all the detail and pattern in nature, in objects and in people. Some artists create photographs that are works of art. Some artists, working from photographs, reproduce them accurately in other media. Other artists use photographs as sketches, gathering ideas and important information or detail. Cameras have become important tools for many contemporary artists.

Computers and related scientific discoveries allow artists to work with new ideas and techniques. Computer images are resources for some artists. Other artists are learning to work with computers to actually produce paintings, designs and other artwork. Graphic designers use computers in their work (television spots and advertisements, layouts, type design, graphic presentation). Industrial designers use computers to design, test and redesign their products, and to design the tools they'll need.

New commercial design techniques and materials include airbrushes, computer-assisted design, graphic tools, plastics, new products and materials. These have been used by some fine artists to create new ways to paint or print their ideas. Combining media and techniques of various types (mixed media and multi-media work) has become common practice.

Contemporary ideas and designs from abroad have influenced our own culture. Automobile designers from Sweden, Germany, Italy and Japan have changed industrial design in America. Furniture designers in Denmark and Italy have influenced our own designers. Fashion designers in France, England and Italy have a strong impact on what American designers create. Fashions, fads, art, life-style and industry (our culture) are all influenced by the artists and designers in other parts of the world.

The *desire to be different*, to be unique, is also an important influence. Artists and designers want their products to stand out. They work hard to create

Robert Cottingham uses cameras to gather visual information. He carefully records this information on canvas. His paintings are direct and powerful reflections of his urban environment. Keen Kottons is a 32" × 32" (81 × 81 cm) oil painting.

American furniture design has been influenced by Scandinavian designers, artists and manufacturers. This Hedensted desk and table are from Denmark. Courtesy Scan, Baltimore.

The design and construction of Japanese and European cars has caused drastic changes in American car design. Courtesy Nissan Motors, Torrance.

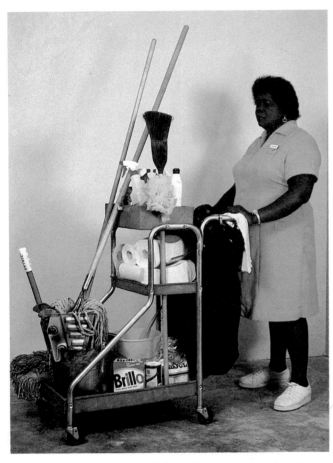

Duane Hanson's very realistic sculpture is directly influenced by his culture, and by new materials, such as plastics, polyvinyls and paints. The figure, Cleaning Woman, *is a lifesize sculpture. The clothing and other objects are real.*

a variety of new results. Many people wish to wear, drive or own something different. So artists are encouraged to pursue new ideas.

Our contemporary lifestyle also influences artists. Some artists show us that we are saturated with multiple images. They create work that repeats a single image. Other artists make large images of common items (soup cans, cigarettes or cereal boxes). Comic strip figures find their way into fine art and advertising. Some artists become our mirror. They criticize our activities and habits. Graphic and industrial design and advertising reflect ideas and concepts of our life-styles.

Religion, nature, social change and *current politics* can all influence an artist's work. Can you suggest how?

In summary, art can change our culture. It can also be changed *by* our culture.

Suggested Activities

1. Artists and designers can be influenced by television, movies, books, sports, travel, seasonal activities and hobbies. Discuss how each may or may not affect fine artists, graphic designers, architects and industrial designers.
2. If your home has strong ethnic or cultural ties, collect art objects or products that reflect these influences. Display or discuss them in class.
3. Look through magazines and cut out illustrations and advertisements that illustrate the influences of cameras, computers and foreign designers on American products or art. Make a bulletin board display or a notebook of your discoveries.
4. How might a universal event or disaster (volcanic eruption, war, peace, famine, tidal wave) influence fine artists? How might they influence graphic and industrial designers? Make drawings, paintings or models to explain your responses.

Creating Art

These students are working on a class mural at Emerson Junior High School, Los Angeles.

9 Drawing

The first recorded drawings were not done on paper but on cave walls in France, Spain and Africa. People have been drawing ever since. However, the materials on which they made their marks have decayed with time, and we cannot see their early sketches. Most drawings before the Middle Ages were drawn to help the painter put colors in the right places. In the early Renaissance, young art students, like you, began drawing from plaster models of ancient sculptures. Their teachers made them copy exactly so they would learn about proportions, shading, lines, shape and form.

In the sixteenth and seventeenth centuries, artists began to keep their drawings as a source book for later work. Some even made drawings to record trips, like an art diary. Their sketches tell us how they saw the world. Such an art diary might be fun for you to make. You might record a summer trip, a class outing or a picnic.

When art returned to classical principles in the nineteenth century, drawing was the most important subject in art schools. Young students spent hours trying to show nature exactly as it appeared. Other artists, however, began to use drawing as a means of personal expression. Their charcoal and ink work became supercharged with energy.

Drawing in the late nineteenth and early twentieth centuries became a more individual way of expressing ideas. Artists began working in their own style. Today, some artists work in detailed and traditional ways, while others use drawing tools to experiment and produce strong individual statements. Contemporary artists might combine drawing with collages, paintings or even three-dimensional forms. In general, however, tools and papers have remained the same.

An industrial designer, working on next year's automobile model, explores ideas using a pencil and a sketchpad. A leading dress designer works on a series of drawings to develop a new line of sportswear.

The landscape architect makes a detailed drawing to show the client how the finished arrangement of plants, trees and rocks will look.

Painters, sculptors, book designers and architects have always begun their work with initial sketches to get ideas flowing.

Michelangelo produced hundreds of drawings before he made his first chisel mark on a block of pure white marble. Leonardo da Vinci in his scientific writings has page after page of drawings (like the doodles in your notebook) from nature and imagination.

Other artists throughout history have left pages or stacks of drawings. Their drawings might be sketches for paintings or sculptures that will follow. But they can also be complete in themselves—framed and displayed as finished art.

One of the most famous drawings in the world is Albrecht Dürer's Praying Hands (1508). It is a sketch in black and white chalk on blue paper. He used the hands of his best friend as a model. Courtesy of the Albertina Museum, Vienna, Austria.

Richard Parker used charcoal and chalk to emphasize form in this untitled, 28" × 22" (71 × 56 cm) drawing. He rubbed the surface gently to obtain the smooth surfaces.

Kerry Strand created Plexus, 25" × 31" (64 × 79 cm), by programming a computer to do the actual drawing. CalComp, Anaheim.

Drawing is as important to an artist, designer or architect as talking is to a speechmaker. Can you imagine a politician that cannot talk? It is just as difficult to think of an artist that cannot draw. Drawing is really the basic activity of art. A good knowledge of drawing will help make other aspects of art easier to understand.

Without looking at your hand, make a drawing of it from memory. Next, look at your hand carefully. Let your eye slowly follow around the edges (contours) of it, noticing the crinkles, overlappings and bulges. Try to make a second drawing that follows the way your eye moves over these contours—slowly and carefully. Your new drawing may not look exactly like your hand (it may be very exaggerated in places), but you have *looked* very carefully. This drawing process has helped you see your hand in a new and more complete way.

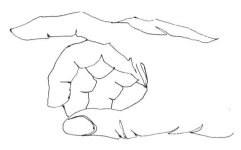

Contour drawings are lines that follow the way your eye moves along the edges of objects.

Richard Wiegmann used various pencils to achieve value contrast in his drawing At The Fair. *Some parts are delicately drawn, while others are boldly shaded.*

Observing and becoming aware of things is what drawing is all about. When you begin to see and draw, you will be following an historical method of recording ideas and thoughts. But you are an individual. When you look at a flower or a cat, you might see it differently than your neighbor (or than Rembrandt, back in the 1600s). Your drawing may be individual and different; that is good.

Tools and Techniques

Pencils are available in many different materials, like graphite, charcoal and carbon. But the first kind is most common. We call it a lead pencil. Lead pencils come in many sizes (large, thin, flat) and intensities (from 6B, the softest and darkest, to 9H, the hardest and lightest). You should experiment to find which you need.

Mistakes in pencil drawing can be erased with several types of erasers. However, some erasers will also chew up the paper, making it difficult to hide corrections. Try to erase as little as possible, especially in quick sketches.

Charcoal is the driest of the dry materials. It comes in several forms: natural sticks, compressed sticks and pencils. Pencils are the cleanest because the material is encased in wood. Like lead pencils, charcoal has a range of values, from soft and dark to hard and light. Charcoal erases easily with a kneaded rubber eraser and can be smeared and smudged with a cloth, fingers or piece of chamois (soft leather cloth). Smudging can be useful in softening edges and blending values (shades of gray). The paper used with charcoal should be textured (try several). Charcoal tends to be messy because of its dryness, and finished work must be sprayed with a fixitive to hold it to the paper. Before starting your drawing, try holding the charcoal in different ways. Try several pressures and papers until you like the result. Sketch

Eugenio Quesada works in many media and styles. His charcoal drawing, Niña Traviesa, *expresses strength through simplicity. This is a characteristic of much Mexican art.*

lightly to begin, and then start the shading and detailing process.

Chalk works like charcoal because it is dry, soft and dusty. Unlike charcoal, it comes in many colors. Finished chalk works also need to be protected with a fixitive. Try dipping the chalk stick into liquid starch before applying it to the paper. The result will be quite unusual and no fixitive is needed. Chalk can also be dipped in water and applied to dry paper, or used dry on wet paper, but fixitives will be needed when it dries.

Wax crayons can be exciting to work with. They combine well with other materials in mixed-media techniques. Points, sides and edges can be used to produce a variety of effects. Fill a page with different lines and textures of a single color. **Rubbings** can be

Anthony van Dyck (seventeenth century) used black and white chalk on gray paper to produce this 20″ (51 cm) study of two heralds. It is part of the painting Procession of Knights of the Garter. He emphasized elaborate costumes, rather than faces. Collection, The Albertina Museum, Vienna, Austria.

Crayon can be a colorful and interesting drawing tool. This imaginative clown is symmetrically balanced. The paper was folded in half to make each side equal, before the artist began.

Bright colors and bold technique make this still life very exciting. It was done with wax crayon. Textures can be shown easily with this drawing medium.

made by placing plain paper over a textured or relief surface and coloring over the paper with the broad side of a crayon. Drawings can then be rubbed with a paper towel or cloth to blend and smooth the crayon tones. Lines can be scratched into the colors with a sharp tool. Can you think of other uses for crayons?

Pen and ink work is similar to drawing with pencils, except that erasing is almost impossible. You must also find ways to produce shading because ink has only one value. Look at some pen and ink sketches to see how cross-hatching, dot patterns and closely-placed lines will give a feeling of shadow or gray. Pen points are available in many different sizes and forms. You should try using several of them. Some points are very fine, others are flat and wide. Although pen and ink drawings are generally black and white, colored inks may be used to add interest to your drawing. Blotting paper or paper towels help pick up unwanted spots and drips. Hard, smooth paper allows clean lines; softer papers give fuzzy lines.

A very fine-tipped pen produced this variety of textures and values. Notice that lines and dots are closer together in dark areas.

113

Brushes can also be used to put ink on paper. The resulting lines and shapes are bold and natural in contrast with the mechanical lines of a pen. Cartoonists often use fine brushes for their drawing because of the thick and thin lines they need.

Wash drawings look like paintings because a brush is used to apply different values. But only a single color is used, so we call them drawings. Make several washes (water with ink added) in containers to provide light, middle and dark values (light, medium and dark gray washes). A full range of values is available if pure ink is used for black and the paper for white. Brush the light values on first, then work to the darker values. Wash drawings make use of drips, slops, spots and splatters to add texture and interest. It is best to work large and on a slanted surface. Use big brushes first and then smaller ones for detail.

Wash drawings use different values of gray washes, applied with various brushes. A stick was used to add ink lines for detail.

This mixed-media drawing combines several markers, colored inks, collage, pencil and contour drawing.

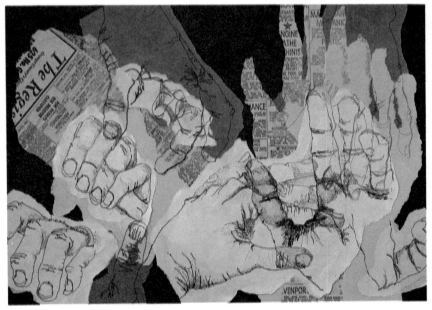

Fiber-tipped markers, fountain pens and ball-point pens can also be used in sketching and drawing. They are clean and easy to use, and they are excellent tools for on-the-spot sketching outdoors. They work well on many different papers, so you should experiment with them. Colors are also available, which might add interest to some projects.

Mixed media, such as wax crayons and transparent ink washes, can produce fascinating textural areas. Other wet and dry materials can also be mixed for exciting results. Make a sketch of charcoal lines and use gray washes over it. Put down some squiggly lines with a warm-colored crayon (orange) and wash over it with a cool-colored watercolor (blue). What other complementary combinations could you use?

Dip the edges of cardboard into ink and draw with this new and different tool. Or scratch away part of your drawing with a razor blade or stencil knife. Take one of your linoleum block prints and use gray or colored washes over it. Can you think of other combinations of wet and dry media that might be exciting? The combinations are endless. Only by experimenting can you see what each grouping of materials can do.

Prepare some washes and have crayon, charcoal, pencils and brushes ready to work. Reach for whatever tool or material seems right at the time. If you are drawing a still life, your drawing can be full of experimental sections and some delightful combinations. Other ideas might not work at all, but this is part of the learning and searching process. Keep trying new combinations.

Learn the strengths and limitations of each material. What do pencils or crayons do best? When you want thin and delicate lines, which drawing tool works best? For large, black areas, what tools would be most convenient to use? As in the other art techniques of sculpture or painting, learn to use the materials and tools that work best for you.

Collage parts combine with pen and black ink to create a fanciful, mixed-media drawing. Notice the way negative spaces are filled with pattern.

Some Design Suggestions

Sitting down with a large piece of blank paper, pencil or charcoal in hand, can produce a feeling of hesitancy. Where do I start? What lines should I make first? Of course, there are many ways to proceed. But a simple three-step plan is easiest.

1. Look at the large shapes first, not at the details. Lightly sketch them in place. This will give you a visual outline in which to work. Keep your outline very simple. Watch for visual relationships between large parts of the subject.
2. Develop your sketch by correcting lines and developing an outline drawing of each subject. Add some major details and arrange the parts in an interesting way.
3. Begin to shade, color or texture, using the material you have selected for the work.

Glance back at the sections on design, and find how the design elements and principles relate to your drawing. Line is the major element used in drawing, but value, space, shape, texture and color are also important. The principles of balance, unity, contrast, emphasis, movement, rhythm and pattern are as important to a good drawing as to jewelry, sculpture or painting. Why is this true? How can contrast be developed in a pencil drawing? How can a crayon drawing make use of pattern?

Look at the range of drawing techniques presented in this book (here and in other sections). As you begin to draw, choose materials that will be best suited for your work. Use paper that will add interest to the drawing. Hints on what to look for are found on the following pages. Experiment with ideas and materials and do not be discouraged when things do not seem to work together. This is the exploration process, and you should learn as much from a failure as from a success.

When you have produced a number of good drawings, you may wish to experiment on your own. You can select your own subject matter, or you may wish to use your drawing tools and materials in different ways. These final drawings may provide a few ideas to get you started. Remember, drawing is just as much seeing and being aware of what you see as it is putting it on paper. So *look carefully*! Take your time, and keep your work simple.

In this sketching technique, the art student has first put down several ink washes in the general shapes of the model. He is now drawing over these washes with a stick and India ink, correcting and adjusting as he draws.

Before creating a finished, shaded pencil drawing of this clarinet section, the student first made several contour sketches. This made the complicated parts more familiar and easier to draw.

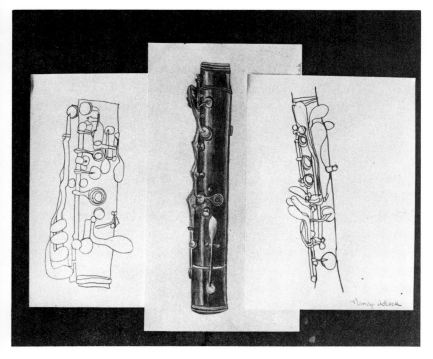

What Can You Draw?

Your art room is full of subjects waiting to be seen and drawn. Your classmates are probably the most available. It might seem hard to draw people, but remember that they are simply subject matter, like boxes or vases. You must look just as carefully at people and record what you see. Do not worry about actual likenesses, but enjoy the process of searching and drawing lines, edges and values.

Posed models are always more exciting if they wear wild costumes, hold things in their hands or are doing something. Put people into still lifes, on top of ladders, under umbrellas, or anything that seems interesting. One day emphasize line, another day concentrate on values and still another day work on action. Check proportions of the figure and face. Note the relative sizes and lengths of various parts.

Also in the art room are objects to group in still life setups. These can range from simple arrangements of three or four objects to complicated groups that cover an entire wall. You might draw the entire still life or only a small part. A strong light helps define objects and cast shadows. Drawings can be realistic, line studies or abstractions. Still lifes offer marvelous subjects for mixed media drawings and experimental work.

Scenes or activities in your own neighborhood—people, workers, shoppers, kids playing, a rainy day, a parade, the local fire engine—provide still more subject matter. Trees, bushes, flowers and animals can be drawn from near or far. You can work from

A group of chairs can provide a subject for drawing. These were first drawn with a contour ink line. The negative space was then brushed in with India ink.

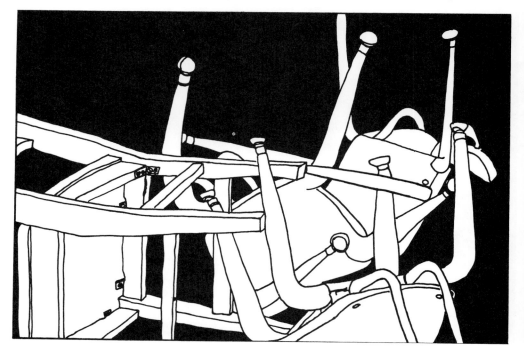

nature, from your surroundings, from reference material or from your memory. The important drawing activities are looking at and recording what you see or remember.

Buildings, automobiles, bicycles, streets, parks, your house and your school are waiting to be drawn. Animals, birds and insects can be drawn at museums, zoos or in your backyard. You can imagine monsters, beautiful scenes, a huge storm, shipwrecks or enchanted castles, and draw them.

You may like to write poetry or descriptive verses. Maybe you could combine your writing with drawing. Experiment with new art forms and fads, with different drawing tools, with different papers or surfaces. The searching and recording process of drawing remains the same even if the subject or material changes.

A student model, still life and plants were sketched in charcoal. The drawing was then shaded and smeared with paper towels. Line was added to sharpen details. Careful erasing brightened the highlights.

Bring a bicycle into class and draw all of it or draw a detailed part. This gear assembly was done in pencil.

Line

How many different kinds of lines can you think of ? Are all lines straight? Or curved? Can a line be thick or thin? Did you ever think of a line as being smooth, jagged, broken, solid, wiggly, or soft and fuzzy? What other kinds of lines are there?

What can be done with line? Is there something that you can describe or express on paper with a line? How about those doodles in your notebook? They were probably done almost entirely with different kinds of line. You should have discovered that you can use a simple element like line to divide a space, to direct the eye (an arrow) or to describe an object. You can use line to make letters, to draw trees and leaves, to represent hair on that cartoon of your teacher and to draw the elephant at the zoo.

Line is probably the most important element of drawing. Think about line. See what effects you can get with various drawing materials.

Using crayon, chalk or pen and ink on paper, create lines that express anger, joy, fear, strength, weakness, speed and slowness.

Create different kinds of lines on paper with unusual drawing tools, such as wire and ink, sticks and ink, cardboard edges and ink. How can these be used in your drawings?

A beautifully clean and crisp line creates the leaf and stem shapes of a classroom plant. Such contour line drawings can describe dozens of things in your classroom.

This contour line drawing was made with pencil. Careful observation was the goal, not an exact likeness.

Use line (pencil or pen and ink or marker) to draw a piece of driftwood. Emphasize the texture and grain in the driftwood.

Draw your own hand, a classmate, or an object with a fine marker on paper. Keep the lines simple and do not worry about erasing any of them.

Write or print your name over and over again on a sheet of typing paper to produce a textural surface. Vary the spaces between words or lines to add variety and contrast.

Other Suggestions

Hold your drawing tools at different places (close to the tip, far back on the pencil). Or hold them differently in your hand (across the palm, between different fingers). See what the new feeling will do for your drawing.

On a wet piece of heavy paper, use a stick and ink line and see what happens. Can you think of subject matter that can make use of this technique?

Use a ballpoint pen and try to express a *feeling* of grass, wood, clouds, wool, concrete, trees or water. Can you think of other things to express this way?

Hold a flower in one hand and make a line drawing of it. Draw what you see and not what you think it should look like. What else can you draw from close up like this?

This line drawing was first done with a thin black marker. Many more lines were added in color with chisel-tipped markers. Can you think of other ways to use this combination of markers and line?

121

Shape

If you draw a line on a piece of paper and move the paper around, ending back where you started, you will have enclosed space. You have made a shape. Is your shape geometric (square, round, triangular) or free-flowing, organic? Shapes can be any of these. They can even be specific like leaves, bottles or faces.

Shapes in drawing can be positive (the objects themselves) or negative (the space around the main objects). Are all shapes outlined with a line? How can you show a flat or solid shape without using line?

Using a pencil, make several tracings of your hands, overlapping the drawing to create new shapes. Shade the shapes you have produced with ink washes of different values and darken all the lines with pen and ink. How else could you fill in the shapes you have created?

On white paper, use a light pencil or charcoal line to sketch the shapes of several objects on a table. Then darken the negative space with chalk or charcoal, leaving the objects white. Can you shade in the negative areas without even putting down sketch lines first?

Cut a shape (animal, leaf, geometric) out of lightweight cardboard. Trace around it over and over again on a sheet of paper to create an overall pattern. Can you think of several ways to arrange the shapes to create an interesting page? How could you fill in the shapes with color?

The leaf and vase shapes were drawn first with a contour ink line. The negative space was inked in black. Parts of the leaf and the vase shapes were then emphasized using shapes cut from newspaper pages. The shapes were fitted and pasted in place.

Only the negative space was shaded to create this still life drawing. If you avoid outlining first, and simply shade the shapes you see, positive shapes remain clean.

A teacher posed while students crayoned contour line drawings. This line searches carefully, but is far from an accurate picture of the teacher. Crayon gives pattern to the shapes.

Other Suggestions

Use the flat side of a crayon to show the shape of different still life objects, one at a time. No detail, just shape. Do not outline first.

Without outlining first, use charcoal (flat sides) and sketch the *shape* of trees and shrubs around school or at home.

Use the flat side of a crayon or charcoal to quickly sketch the *shape* of student models. Each model should pose for only two or three minutes.

Richard Parker uses charcoal and chalk so that simple value areas become powerful, dramatic forms. The large size of the drawing, 28" × 22" (72 × 56 cm), makes the forms monumental. Can you use this concept to make a value drawing of simple forms?

Value and Form

Value is the darkness or lightness in a drawing. What would the darkest possible value be? Or the lightest? Which values, dark or light, may seem gloomy and dramatic? Which values would you use to show something delicate? Between black and white, how many values of gray can be created?

By using various values (grays) in a drawing, you can create shading, which gives a feeling of form and depth. Look at the shading on a rounded object in a strong light. Is the change from light to dark values gradual and slow or sharp and quick? What difference is there in the shadow pattern of a rectangular box or block? Is the shadow pattern on an organic or irregular object likely to be gradual or quick? Experiment with the light from a slide projector and several different objects. How can this knowledge be useful in drawing still life objects or people's faces?

Other Suggestions

Paste a small black and white photograph (from a magazine) on a large sheet of drawing paper. Use a pencil drawing to explode the photograph in all directions, continuing the lines and values for several inches.

On brown or gray construction paper, use black and white chalk to draw a simple still life of several objects under a strong single light. Shade carefully to show roundness or squareness and value changes. The paper itself will be the middle values while the white and black chalk will provide the light and dark values.

Use charcoal and drawing paper to make a value study of several smooth bottles. Rub the drawing with a cloth or chamois to smooth the charcoal and make it appear glasslike.

Brown construction paper provides the middle values in this simple still life. White and black chalk add the other values.

In this student wash drawing, the values include many grays in the range from black to white. The shading creates a feeling of three-dimensional form.

The central black and white magazine photograph was expanded and shaded with pencil. The values and forms continue for several inches.

Pen and ink were used to create an impression of texture. Study these for technique, and create your own system for making a textural page.

Textures and Patterns

Rub your left hand over this page in your book and your right hand over your clothes. What differences do you feel? How does tree bark feel? Or rounded pebbles? Or glass? Or carpet? Or a cat's fur? To which of your senses does *texture* appeal?

Do you think it is possible to create a *sense* of texture without being able to actually feel it? Can photographers do this? Can artists? Can you?

Patterns are repeated lines, shapes or colors in art. They often create a feeling of texture. Can you notice several patterns in your room or in your classmates' clothes? In a drawing, can you think of ways that patterns can be used to fill negative or positive space?

Make **rubbings** of various textures around school (inside or out) by placing paper (bond or typing) over textures and rubbing the paper with the side of a crayon. Use some contrasting colors over the same

A student carefully observed the texture and grain of a piece of driftwood. The observations are recorded in pen and ink.

These simple bottle shapes were first drawn in black ink on construction paper. White chalk was then added to some of the shapes. The background was made by placing the paper on different textural surfaces and rubbing black crayon over it.

This furry dog was "drawn" with finger prints. Can you think of other ways to use "printing" to help texture your drawing?

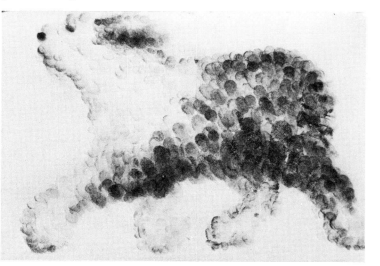

rubbing. Sometimes, a colored wash of watercolor in a complementary or contrasting color will emphasize the feeling of texture. When you have many textures, cut them up and paste together a bird or animal.

Other Suggestions

Fill a page with some drawn textures, such as tree bark, sand, bricks, leaves, wood or glass. Use only one drawing material, such as a fibertipped pen or pencil.

Make an outline drawing of the parts of a machine (typewriter, bicycle, motor) and fill in the spaces with various patterns. Use pen and ink and try to make each patterned area different. Do not try for realism.

Make a line drawing of natural subject matter (tree branches, flowers, animals). Divide them into smaller shapes and fill each shape with a different pattern. Would brush lines be better than pencil or pen lines?

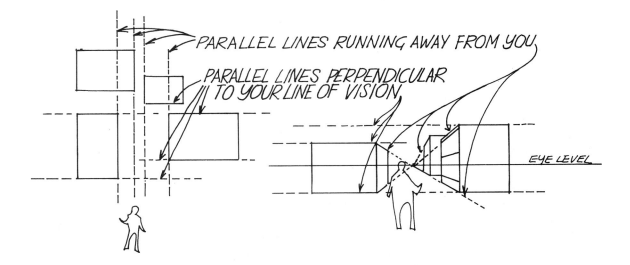

PARALLEL LINES RUNNING AWAY FROM YOU

PARALLEL LINES PERPENDICULAR TO YOUR LINE OF VISION

EYE LEVEL

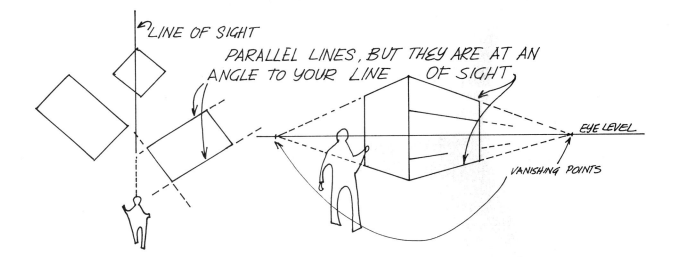

LINE OF SIGHT

PARALLEL LINES, BUT THEY ARE AT AN ANGLE TO YOUR LINE OF SIGHT

EYE LEVEL

VANISHING POINTS

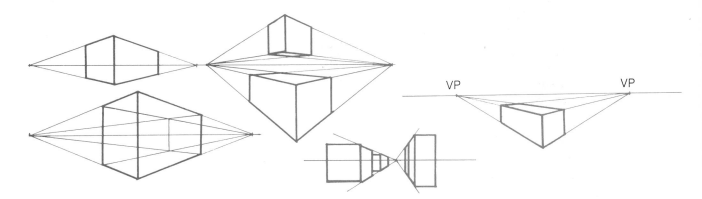

VP   VP

128

Space and Perspective

Depth, or a feeling of space, can be shown on a flat surface in several ways:

1. By overlapping some of the objects, so one appears to be behind another;
2. By shading objects and allowing them to cast shadows;
3. By showing, if you are above the objects in a still life, the base of the item nearest to you as the lowest in the drawing;
4. By drawing a person farther away smaller than the person right next to you; the same goes for animals, apples and trees.

Look at photographs in magazines. Notice how the techniques listed above give the feeling of depth on a flat surface.

When you try to make rounded or blockish forms appear three-dimensional in your drawing, the process is called **perspective drawing**. All the methods described above will help achieve that feeling, but there are other ways as well. One is called *linear perspective* , and uses lines to show depth. Parallel straight lines that run away from you seem to meet (converge) at a point called the *vanishing point* Why do you think it is given that name? Close one eye so you can see like a single-lens camera. Observe all the parallel lines around you—ceiling tiles, floor tiles or boards, lockers, rows of windows. Notice how the lines converge as they get farther away from you. If they continued past the end of the room, what would eventually happen to them?

If the building or boxes are square to your line of sight, only one vanishing point is needed. This is called *one-point perspective* (see Diagram A). But if the boxes are sitting at an odd angle to your line of sight, *two-point perspective* is needed (see Diagram B).

Draw an *eye-level line* across your page. This is the level of your eye from where you are standing. Put a vanishing point at about the center of the line. Put a square or rectangle on the page (above, below or across the eye level). Draw lines from the corners of the square to the vanishing point. Use a ruler to keep the lines straight. To limit the depth of the form, draw lines *parallel* to the horizontal lines of the original square. This will produce a box form. Try other locations on the page. Try making the boxes seem transparent. Can you shade the box forms as though light were coming from a single source? Use diagrams A and C for help.

Draw an eye-level line across the page and place vanishing points at either end. Draw a single vertical line (of an inch or two) crossing the eye level. Make lines from the top and bottom of this line to the vanishing points. Limit the depth of the box by making two vertical lines on the way to the vanishing points. Darken only the lines of the form. Use diagrams B and C for help.

Draw an eye-level line across the page and place vanishing points at each end. Make the first vertical line below the eye level and again draw lines to the two vanishing points. Limit the depth of the form with two vertical lines and draw a line to each vanishing point from the top of these lines. Darken the lines of the three-dimensional form to make it stand out from the rest of the lines.

Draw similar forms above the eye level. Can you shade the forms to strengthen the feeling of depth?

Remember that all vertical lines are straight up and down. *All horizontal lines* **must** go to one of the two vanishing points.

A cylinder is round only when you look directly into it. The circular opening becomes a flatter oval as the rim tips and approaches the eye level. Notice the same thing with dishes, wheels and similar objects.

Eye level

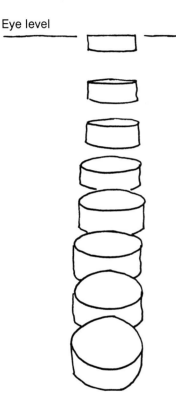

Cylinders have round openings. You can see this as you look through them. But, as you tilt a cylinder down so that you are looking across the opening instead of through it, the opening seems to become flatter and more oval shaped until it becomes completely flat at eye level. See Diagram D for a visual explanation.

Other Suggestions
Draw a simple house shape in perspective. Add windows and doors and landscaping.

Make a landscape drawing with trees. Show depth by changing the sizes of trees as they go off into the distance.

Draw several flat geometric shapes, making them appear to overlap. Shade the one closest to you with the darkest pencil shade. Have the shapes appear lighter as they get farther away.

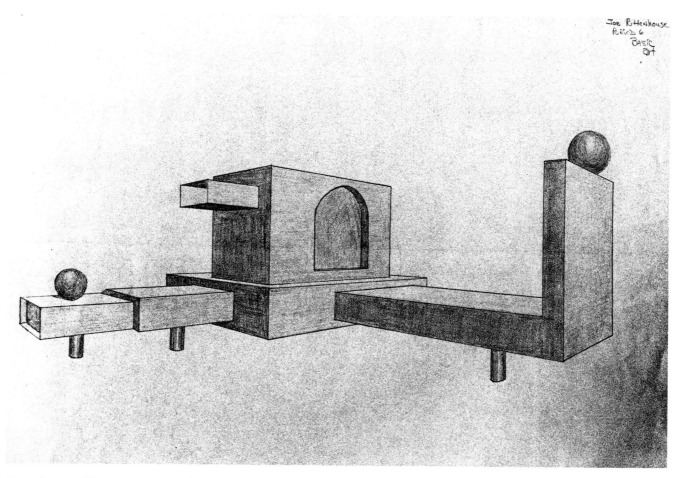

Joe Rittenhouse
Period 6
Basic
Art

Experiment with perspective and create a set-up of boxes and spheres. Note how shading helps the illusion of depth and space. This shading implies that light is coming from a single source.

This student has used shading, overlapping and placement of the nearest object lowest in the picture. These techniques give the illusion of depth and space in this wash drawing.

Using Letters and Words

ZOOM!   SWISH   THWACK!!!
GURGLE . . .   ZING!

Do such words bring pictures to your mind? Could you letter such words to make them *look* like what they say? Commercial designers and comic strip artists often draw such words to give them visual emphasis. Can you letter words that say and look like:

storm   mist   flight
waterfall   heavy   quick

You can also have the words make images or pictures of what they say. Both uppercase (capital) and lowercase (body or small) letters are used.

Bull   Manhattan   Flower
Pineapple   Thistle

Can you think of others?

Words can be arranged to produce designs or picture images. Or you might try mixing words and numbers together, like 8ight or 5IVE. You can design a special monogram using your initials. Or use all the letters of your name to produce a designed page. Many sketches on scratch paper are usually needed before the design idea is ready to paint. Tempera, crayon, pastels, colored ink or watercolor can be used in such work.

Draw with pencil, and then use tempera paint to create a 9″×12″ (23 × 30 cm) design using your name. Perhaps you could work in a circular design with a 9″ (23 cm) diameter.

Pick one or more of the suggested words (or think of your own) and letter the word, while also creating a visual picture. Use watercolor, pen and ink or markers to complete the work.

Janet designed her name to produce a house shape. She cut the letters from lightweight cardboard and covered them with aluminum foil.

The letters of your name (or any word) can be designed and outlined in pencil. Then filled in with pen and ink patterns.

Scratching Out

Almost all two-dimensional art is concerned with adding color or value to the surface. But to get interesting results, color can be scratched off again. **Crayon etching** is one method that uses scratching techniques to finish the work.

On white tagboard, apply a *heavy* coating of wax crayon in abstract patterns or shapes. Brush a coat of India ink or black tempera paint over the entire surface and allow to dry. (If the ink doesn't cover, rub a little talcum powder on the crayon surface before inking.) Using a sharp tool (such as a compass point or needle), draw lines in the black surface to reveal the crayon color beneath. Which colors will show best through the black ink? Large areas can be scratched with a dull knife. What other tools might be used to create lines or shapes?

On a textured surface (heavy drawing paper, pebble board), make a drawing of a portrait or a still life. Color it *heavily* with wax crayon. Cover the entire surface with India ink. When dry, use a dull razor blade or knife to remove most of the ink. Some ink will remain in the low spots on the textured surface, giving the entire sheet an ancient look. Can you think of some textured papers that would add interest to this project?

A crayon etching is the colorful background for these active bugs and spiders. The black thick-and-thin outlines are not removed.

This imaginary structure was created by scratching from the surface of a crayon etching.

Other Suggestions

Use white tempera instead of black for a completely different effect. Does this give you more ideas? What colors might you use for a jungle scene?

Geometric designs, made with a ruler and a compass, can produce interesting compositions. How can you use a design that has a crayon and scratching process to increase interest?

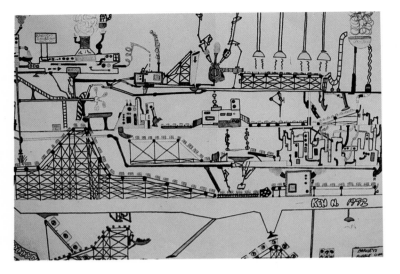

Ink, colored markers and imagination went into designing and drawing this factory. Machines, robots and conveyor belts are part of the production line here. Does this give you new drawing ideas?

You can create a collage using parts of black and white magazine pictures. Create a humorous situation. Use a pencil to fill in the blanks with patterns and values.

Wax crayon, rubbings, collage and ink are combined to create an inventive machine. Can you think of ways to combine similar media and create other machines, fantasy animals or people?

This pen and ink drawing uses many different shapes. The real focus is the dozens of patterns that fill the spaces. In many places, pattern gives the appearance of texture.

Trade names and logos were drawn with heavy wax crayon and arranged like city lights at night. Watercolor washes were then brushed over the sheet to provide a background for the crayon work. Could this wax-resist technique be used for drawing flowers, athletes or animals?

137

10 Painting

An artist's painting can be an explosion of color, soft colors used together or circles, squares and triangles of color. It can be colored views of nature. A painting can be made with soft colors (as some portraits are), harsh contrasts of color or juicy, joyful colors.

Although all these paintings might have different subject matter and style, what do they have in common? How does painting differ from drawing? How is it similar to drawing or sculpture?

When people hear the word art, they often think of painting first. That is natural, because painting has been a very popular art form for a long time. Painters have recorded people's joys and sufferings. They have shown what people thought. They have described real and imaginary landscapes, explored the form and color of ordinary things. They have expressed feelings about religion, inspired revolutions and shared their delight in color and light.

Leonardo da Vinci felt that painting was the supreme art, because a painter created the *illusion* or *feeling* of reality and depth where none really existed. Leonardo thought that if he could convince the viewer that the subject of the painting was real, his painting was successful. Today, many painters disagree with Leonardo's feelings about art. But even in

an era of artistic experimentation, painting is still an important means of expression.

In ancient times, paintings told stories of mythology and later of religious heroes and of the Bible. Renaissance painters wanted to paint in the most realistic way possible. Later the emphasis moved to action, light, playfulness, drama, adventure and even protest. But the artists still painted people, places and things. In the late nineteenth and early twentieth centuries the emphasis shifted to color, design and personal statements. The paintings themselves became more important than their subjects.

Today, painting is both realistic (using objects we know) and nonobjective (not showing familiar objects). It can be as geometric (using circles, squares, triangles) as an arithmetic problem; as free-form as a storm. Paintings can be colorful, dull, large, tiny, realistic. They can be emotional, almost invisible or carefully done on walls, canvas, glass, plastic or pavement. Renaissance artists were all trying to do the same things in their work. Artists of today are heading in many directions, communicating in their own ways. What effect does this idea have on the way you produce your own artwork or make visual statements?

Thousands of years separate the lives of the two artists whose work is shown here. Yet the paintings of the unknown cave artist (10,000 B.C.) and Veloy Vigil (1983 A.D.) have much in common. Both painted subjects they knew very well. They used color in personal ways and painted to communicate their ideas. The cave painting is from Lascaux, France. *Sunbow,* by Veloy Vigil is acrylic, 72" × 90" (182 × 228 cm).

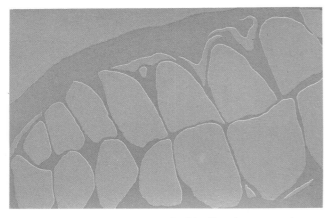

Brilliant tempera colors, applied in flat shapes, make a crisp, clean painting. A limited palette of two colors is effective to enlarge a close-up view of teeth. This view is from a black and white photograph.

The artist used to set up the design motif for this painting. The repeated shapes were then carefully painted with tempera.

Materials, Tools and Techniques

In the past, painting generally referred to oils and watercolors. While these are the usual materials, today's artists have many others from which to choose: acrylics, casein, tempera, gouache, lacquer, enamel, alkyds and some experimental materials.

The most common paints used in schools are tempera and transparent watercolor. Both of these are thinned and cleaned with water. Tempera is opaque (you cannot see through it), while watercolor is transparent, allowing you to see through several layers to colors and lines underneath.

Tempera paint is a liquid, generally as thick as thick cream. It brushes easily and dries quickly to a dull matte (not glossy) finish. You can mix tempera easily in flat trays. To lighten the value of colors, add white; to darken values, add black. When tempera is thinned with water it becomes slightly transparent but chalky. Tempera colors are bright, strong and can be covered easily. However, if you scrub too hard with your brush, the layers underneath will loosen and mix with the top layer. Both bristle and soft hair brushes (camel, squirrel) work well with tempera.

Transparent **watercolor** comes in tubes or pans. Generally, soft brushes are used to flow the color onto paper, after mixing it with water in a tray or dish. Because you can see through the colors, you can build a rich surface by using layer after layer of color. Apply a new layer of paint only when the other layers are completely dry. Otherwise a running mixture will occur. Experiment with these mixtures, because they can be used in future paintings.

To use watercolor, rub a color in the watercolor pan with a wet brush and use the brush to color the water in your tray. This thinned watercolor is called a **wash**. Brush the wash onto the paper, using the lightest colors first. Because they are transparent, light-colored washes will not cover dark areas. There

The opaque quality of tempera (left) and the transparent quality of watercolor (right) can be compared in these two student paintings. Notice how the thick and thin black line of the tempera painting differs from the consistent line in the painting on the previous page.

Transparent watercolor paintings usually have a light feeling. Artists use watercolor brushes freely and stress the transparency of the paint. Winslow Homer's Sloop, Bermuda *shows many of the spontaneous qualities of watercolor. The paper is left unpainted where the artist wants white. The Metropolitan Museum of Art (Amelia B. Lazarus Fund).*

is no white color in transparent paint. So to get a light pink, you must mix more *water* with red, and use it on white paper. The white of the paper shows through the thinned paint to produce pink. If you need white in your watercolor painting, you must leave the white paper blank in those places.

Most paints are made to be applied with **brushes** of various types—bristle, squirrel hair, sable or synthetic fibers. But painting knives, rollers, sponges or cardboard may also be used.

The surface on which you paint is called the **ground**, and it is often some type of paper. Water-based paints, such as watercolor, tempera, alkyds and acrylics, can be used on papers of various thicknesses or textures. Oil paints are usually put on canvas, but they can also be used on paper. Masonite or pressed board, coated once or twice with white gesso, are excellent surfaces for painting with oils, acrylics or tempera.

Before the twentieth century, artists experimented mainly with subject matter—how to organize a landscape, place things in a still life or pose a model. When Pablo Picasso and Georges Braque began gluing paper on their paintings however, new doors were opened for experimentation.

Today, there are no restrictions on working methods or materials. You can wash color away, scratch it out or spray it on. You can glue materials to your paintings, shape the canvas or paint on three-dimensional surfaces. Or you can devise your own experiments.

To insure simplicity, transparent watercolor was applied with a single, flat brush. Colors were mixed before painting and were not applied over each other. White areas are unpainted paper.

Juicy washes of watercolor were laid on the paper. When the sheet was dry, imaginary animals and faces were drawn in black line on the colored surface.

Shells, sand dollars and starfish form the patterns for this design, carried out in a few bright colors. The artist applied crayon first, then washed over it with tempera. Designs were scratched through the tempera, and watercolor and ink were then brushed on the surface.

Resist techniques give interesting textures and create many fascinating effects. If you apply wax crayon very heavily on paper and brush thinned watercolor washes over the marks, the wax resists the water. The watercolor only colors the background paper. The most exciting results happen if the wash is a complementary color (or darker valued color) of the crayon's color.

You can create another resist technique by drawing with (or dribbling) rubber cement on paper. When the cement is dry, paint over the entire surface with watercolors in any pattern or color. When the paint is dry, rub the rubber cement off with your fin-

gers. The clean paper will show through in a pattern of lines. You may also dribble PVA glue (white glue) first. It too will resist watercolor, but it cannot be rubbed off when dry. The patterns that the glue makes may give you ideas for how to finish your work. Any greasy substance will resist any watery substance, so you may be able to think of a few other resist techniques.

Washing out colors is another way to create textural surfaces. Brush tempera paint (any color) on paper in a line or pattern. Leave the plain paper exposed in many places. When the paint is dry, cover the entire sheet with a layer of India ink, applied with a soft brush. When this is dry, hold the sheet under running water and wash the surface. The tempera areas will come loose. The line you painted will be left as clear paper, and the original background will be black ink.

When several techniques or materials are used in a painting, it is called a **mixed media painting**. Think of ways to use various materials and techniques in mixed media paintings.

You have pasted paper before, but maybe you didn't call it a **collage**. Pasting paper to create artwork is rather new. Pablo Picasso did it for the first time in 1912. Since then, many students and artists have found ways to paste paper in their work.

You can make collages without using any paint at all. Just paste paper or cloth, using them instead of paints. Collages can be made with flat colors (like construction paper or tissue paper) or with images and colors cut from magazines. Can you think of other materials, besides paper, that might be used in a collage?

Paper and canvas are not the only grounds or painting surfaces. While most painting surfaces are flat, you may also work on shaped, irregular or three-dimensional surfaces. Artists may put objects or forms behind their canvas to produce bulges or tentlike projections. Paper shapes (like cones, cubes, pie plates) can be glued to heavy cardboard and a painting done over the entire surface. You may even want to do a nonobjective or abstract painting around a cube, rectangular box or cylinder that you find or build. Forms of all types (plaster, metal, wood, cardboard, Styrofoam or plastic) can be the ground for a painting.

Using simple materials and tools, there are many ways you can experiment. The following pages explore some of them, but you may think of new ideas of your own.

Create an ancient look. Make a still life with flat tempera paint and cover it with India ink. After this, wash the painting under a faucet. Use black crayon to outline and help redefine the original shapes.

Design Suggestions

Begin a painting in the same way as you would begin a drawing. Sketch the largest shapes first, lightly, to organize the major elements. Place the objects with care. If you will be using transparent paint (watercolor, thinned acrylics or tempera), you might want to make a detailed drawing. If you use opaque paints (oils, tempera or thick acrylics), paint the largest shapes first, with large brushes. Later, add detail using smaller brushes. Opaque paints cover what is underneath them, so detailed drawing is usually wasted.

Painters use all the elements of design (line, color, value, texture, space, shape and form). Study several of the paintings in this book to see how the artists used each element.

The principles of design (balance, unity, contrast, pattern, emphasis, movement and rhythm) are used in every art form, and painting is no exception. Paul Cézanne's or Edward Hopper's paintings show how all the principles can be used to produce a strong and carefully designed painting. Look in the section on design to refresh your memory; notice some of the examples there. As you work on your own paintings, these principles will help you solve problems. Your paintings will show better design.

Still Life with Apples and Peaches, *Paul Cézanne. Collection, The National Gallery of Art, Washington, D.C. (gift of Eugene and Agnes Meyer).*

Edward Hopper painted Lighthouse Hill *in his strong, simple style. It is a lesson in design. Eye movement begins in the lower right corner and leads up to the left and back to the house; then on to the lighthouse piercing the sky. The dark cap of the tower and the wisps of white clouds keep your eye from leaving the picture. You can see contrast in value and shape. Emphasis is developed through contrast and simplicity. Feel the rhythm as your eye goes over the rounded hill forms. See the asymmetrical balance the artist achieves with shape and value. Hills and textures form patterns of repeated shapes. Consistent brush strokes and simple shapes provide unity. Can you find line, shape, value, texture and space in the painting? Collection of the Dallas Museum of Fine Arts (gift of Mr. and Mrs. Maurice Purnell).*

The Importance of Color

What is the color of a sunset? Of ice? Of cool forests? Of fire? Does the idea of happiness bring a color to your mind? What colors show anger? Sorrow? Can some colors be happy or sad? Violent or gentle?

Can colors express feelings? How can this idea help you in painting?

Is the ocean always blue? What might cause it to change color in nature? Why might an artist want to paint water red or green? Can you think of a reason why an artist might paint the sky green or brown?

Look back to the discussion on color. Refresh your memory about primary and secondary colors; hue, value and intensity; and complementary colors.

Do you think you could create an entire painting using only one color and black and white? This would be called a *monochromatic painting* because only a single color is used.

This monochromatic painting is part of a large still life with a manikin. One color, black and white are the only tempera paints used. Notice the variety of values that the student created.

LeRoy Nieman uses vivid colors that are not realistic, but communicate excitement. The contrasting colors and intensities in Hank Aaron make a powerful statement.

Only two colors and black and white are used in Frederick Hammersley's carefully-designed oil painting. The painting technique used in Whether Vane, 45" × 45" centimeters (114 × 114 cm), is completely different from the other examples on these two pages.

In Janet Fish's oil painting, Red Pitcher and Black Vases, 1980, 54" × 84" (138 × 214 cm), the artist uses primary and secondary colors. Notice how the complementary hues create dramatic contrasts. What effect does the black have on the painting? Robert Miller Gallery, New York.

What Can You Paint?

Once you decide you want to paint, you may ask questions such as "What can I paint? How should I paint it?"

Review the section in the chapter on drawing that deals with subject matter. Artists work best when they know their subject matter. So think about personal experience or things you have seen. Express your own view or feelings about these things.

How about your imagination? Have you imagined glorious victories in sports, or magical events? What if you could fly, or swim for miles under the sea? Stretch your imagination. Think about dangerous jobs, things that cannot really happen, wild storms. All these ideas could be used to make a painting.

Mary Cassatt painted Woman Reading, *31" × 25" (79 × 63 cm), to portray her sister Lydia doing something she enjoyed. Cassatt's colors are warm. Her brush strokes are loose and soft. The Norton Simon Foundation, Los Angeles.*

Richard Diebenkorn plays large areas of light value against small areas of intense color. Many of his abstract oil paintings show this technique. Ocean Park Series #49, 93" × 81" (236 × 206 cm). Los Angeles County Museum of Art.

Robert Cottingham paints his urban environment exactly as it would appear in photographs. His neon signs, plastic, glass and metal usually are seen in bright sunlight. *Starr* is acrylic on paper, 16.5" × 8" × 24.5" (40 × 20 × 63 cm).

Search your memory for other ideas. Do you remember summer vacations, your first swim in the ocean, a scary roller coaster ride, a trip to the zoo? Your memory can provide some exciting material.

Can trash cans, roller skates, your own front door, brick walks or picket fences be the subject matter of a painting? Look carefully at things around you—folds in cloth, tree bark, wood, peeling paint. The more carefully you look at your world, the more subject matter you will find for your paintings.

Can you paint abstract things? How can you paint anger, love or suffering? Can happiness or sadness be shown visually? What other feelings might make good subjects?

As you can see, there is really no limit to *what* to paint. But you might wonder *how* to paint it. Look at the work of other artists. Their paintings will show how they thought about their subjects.

Some artists have painted battle scenes to show how good it is to win. Others show how cruel war is. You may want to say something in your painting *about* the subject. How can you describe a glass bottle? Is it smooth or colored? Does it reflect things? Could you also show an adventure story about the bottle? Could you draw a cartoon using it? Think about what it is used for. Could you show it in a trash pile, or littering the landscape?

Think about these ideas when you think of other objects, too. How do you feel about your street? About war or slavery? About school, basketball or hunting? Your feelings will help you decide how you will paint, what colors you will use, how you will arrange the parts of the painting and even how you will brush the colors.

What you say and how you say it may be different from what your classmates say. Yet all are worthwhile statements. You must keep looking, seeing, feeling and painting to develop your own style.

Painting People Around Us

Throughout history, artists have painted people. Some were heroes while others were friends of the artist. Some artists painted models while others painted from memory. Perhaps you can think of reasons why so many paintings in the past have been about people.

Some such paintings are realistic, some imaginary, some cartoons. Some are portraits (paintings of faces) of friends, kings, queens or other important people. Others are self-portraits (paintings of the artists themselves). Many show the full figures of people in their environments.

It is not always necessary to paint a picture that looks exactly like the person you are painting. Sometimes the feeling or action of the painting is more important than the person. Perhaps you want to show people working hard. You may use models in working poses to draw from, but it is not important that the faces or bodies in the painting look exactly like the ones you see. You may even use a human face as a design or in a cartoon, and it may not look real at all.

To keep the proportions of the figure correct (if that is important), compare the size of one feature with the size of other features. Notice how big the hands are compared with the face. Check the length of the arms on the body, or compare the hip-to-knee distance with the knee-to-ankle distance.

To paint a classmate in a standing or walking pose, do not sketch first. Use a large brush and a single tempera color. Paint only the *shape* of the model. Then make another painting. With a single color, paint only the background (negative space) around the subject, leaving the figure blank. Paint your subjects large. How can you use this technique to express *action*? Can you use the tempera and ink washing-out technique with this subject matter?

The ceramics teacher posed in a working position for student sketches. Students later painted the sketches with tempera in complementary colors and black and white.

152

Personal style is evident and recognizable in these two paintings, both of which contain figures. Notice the Indian in Veloy Vigil's Moccasin Bead, acrylic, 36" × 36" (91 × 91 cm). It is stylized and simplified to fit the artist's design concept. Robert Vickrey painted a girl and her kitten in Bubbles, egg tempera, 31" × 43" (79 × 109 cm). His space is carefully designed with attention to natural back lighting. He has frozen a moment in time. Courtesy Hirschl & Adler Galleries.

With your teacher or a classmate posing in a "working" position (as a carpenter, plumber, painter, sculptor or something similar), make a sketch in pencil that almost fills the paper. Use tempera paint in just a few colors (a primary color and its complementary hue, plus black and white) to finish the painting. Put in your own background or environment. Do not try to produce a likeness of the model. Try to paint the *activity* you see.

Look through magazines for advertisements or photos that tell something about your interests, studies, thoughts or dreams. Before you make a collage of them on cardboard, cut out a silhouette outline of yourself. Have a classmate trace your shadow. (You can cast your shadow on construction paper by using a flashlight or the light from a projector.) Use both the cut-out silhouette and your material from the magazines to produce a large collage. Use rubber cement or white glue to paste the paper to cardboard.

A flashlight made a silhouette which a student traced on construction paper. That "portrait," along with magazine cutouts that show the student's interests, make an interesting collage.

Three costumed figures were drawn with simple lines and then watercolored. A heavy ink line was brushed on to add strength and definition. The finished student work is both simple and powerful.

Other Suggestions

Draw, in pencil, a classmate model dressed in a fantastic costume. Then go over the lines heavily with white or colored crayon. Use watercolor washes (color and water) to paint the picture. Try to catch the feeling and effect of the costume, even in the painted background.

You may select an active sports player for your subject. Wet a sheet of paper with a sponge. While it is still wet, flow watercolor washes onto it in the **general shape** of the athlete. Let the colors run together. When the paper is dry, use wax crayons to add detail and outline where you might need it. Emphasize the action and activity, not the person.

It takes experience to select simple shapes to paint. William Pajaud's watercolor, Southern Fisherman, *is a perfect example of simple strength. Large shapes were put down first. Several simple textures complete the work.*

Painting a Still Life

Arrange a tall green bottle, two red apples, a cracked jug, a lemon and a bit of patterned orange cloth on a table. When you draw or paint it, it is called a *still life* . Artists, in the past hundred years, have used such arrangements in realistic, carefully designed, nonobjective, broken up or experimental ways.

Paul Cézanne painted wonderful still lifes. Pablo Picasso, Juan Gris and other cubists fractured still life

Juan Gris broke up the elements in his still life and rearranged them to paint Still Life with a Poem *(1915). Oil, 32" × 25" (81 × 46 cm), Norton Simon Foundation.*

William Harnett painted still lifes that give the illusion of reality. Munich Still Life *(1882) is a Super Realistic painting that fools your eye. Dallas Museum of Fine Arts (Dallas Art Association Purchase).*

objects and rearranged the parts to suit their design. Today, students and artists all over the world work from still lifes to discover shape and color, to work with line and value and to experiment with new techniques and styles. Why do you think still life is used for all these artistic activities?

You can arrange your own still lifes by using five (or more) objects of different sizes, shapes and colors. It will be a more interesting painting if you group the items together. You may put the objects against a cloth or colored paper backing or create your own background in the painting.

Stand the objects in a row on the table. Using a pencil, draw the *outline* (contour) of one object quite large in the center of the page. Then outline a second item, partly overlapping the first. Draw a third

This painting is part of a larger still life. Notice the full range of colors, combined with contrasting values. The runs and puddles which occur on drawing paper are well used here.

A student designed this still life by overlapping the shapes of several objects. The student painted and textured the surface, then outlined with a thick and a thin line.

Crayon and tempera combine to make a vivid still life. This one emphasizes warm and cool colors.

157

Objects in this still life were first sketched in pencil, and then painted using only white and black tempera, mixed to make a variety of grays. Black crayon, rubbed over some areas, emphasizes the painted texture. Can this technique be used with limited colors as well?

shape, overlapping each or both of the previous shapes. Let the objects show through each other. Draw all the objects in this way. Then, use tempera paint to color the *shapes.* Paint the created shapes and not the objects themselves. Can you think of ways to get a flat background that will not overpower the positive shapes? Finish the design by painting a heavy black line around each color, like a stained glass window.

You can also arrange a simple still life of objects that are placed together. Draw the arrangement with pencil and show how one object is behind another by overlapping them, but let them appear solid. Using only warm colors of tempera (or only cool colors), paint the entire page. Choose your own colors, not those of the actual objects. When the paint is dry, outline the shapes with a heavy black tempera line. Rub the side of a black crayon lightly over the surface to emphasize the texture of the paint and to give a feeling of unity.

On the textured paper (oatmeal paper) or cardboard (matboard), sketch a still life. Paint flat shapes with tempera paint. Do not be concerned with shading or values. When dry, cover the entire surface with slightly thinned India ink and a soft brush. When that dries (overnight), hold the painting under a faucet and rinse away most of the tempera and ink. Stop when an interesting "ancient" look appears. When the paper dries, use a black crayon to outline, shade or finish in some way.

Other Suggestions

Draw a bouquet of flowers (real or artificial) with a heavy wax crayon to express the feeling of color and texture. Fill the page with color and crayon. When you're done, use watercolor washes of various cool or contrasting colors (including black) over the surface. Emphasize contrasts by adding more and deeper washes until you are happy with the color and texture.

Using a simple still life arrangement (or a small part of a large and complicated arrangement), fill the page with a line pencil drawing. Simplify the lines by drawing over them with a heavy black ink or tempera line. Use tempera paint to finish the work. Let the new colors partly cover the black lines so that they almost disappear in places. Try to produce shading effects and highlights (the places where the brightest lights are seen). What would you mix with colors to darken their values? Or lighten them? You may use a full range of color, or use only warm, only cool or one color and its complement.

Crayon resist technique calls attention to the bright splashes of color in the flowers. The student used wax crayons and watercolor on oatmeal paper.

Tissue paper was first glued to white paper. Then flower shapes were cut and the centers painted in. These were then glued to another surface and the vase and background were painted. Does this give you new ideas for still lifes?

A student painted this watercolor landscape by visually recalling part of a summer trip.

A young artist created this strong statement about environmental pollution. It is not difficult to get the message.

Painting Your Environment

Where do you live? Do you live in the country or in the city? Have you seen mountains? Oceans? A rushing stream? Or rushing people in a big city? What other kinds of environments might you see? Your environment surrounds you wherever you go, and it is constantly changing. Paintings of the natural environment are called **landscapes**. Urban scenes are called **cityscapes**. What would you call a painting of the ocean?

Your environment doesn't mean only areas of land. It also means individual flowers or leaves. It means not only big-city skylines but also a window or

The stylized buildings in this tempera cityscape (right) emphasize the crowding in a city.

porch. You can paint your environment from a distance or from close up.

What colors might you use to paint a desert landscape, a tropical jungle or a mountain in winter? How can colors help you say what you want to say about your surroundings? When might you add people?

Using tempera or watercolor, paint part of your environment at school. Make several pencil sketches of buildings, the practice field, a classroom or the main entrance. Your painting should try to say something about your school. Use colors that are realistic, or those that emphasize your feelings about the school environment.

Create a cityscape by stressing the glitter and excitement of the lights and signs at night. Fill a white sheet of paper with heavily applied crayons in bright colors and white. Spell out words and show the designs of neon lights and billboards. Can magazines give you some ideas for signs? Perhaps you can use signs from your town in this imaginary composition. When the page is full, mix **very dark** watercolor washes (black and dark blue, for example) and brush them over the page. Watch what happens as the crayon resists the water. It might take several washes to produce the feeling of night, with bright crayon lights shining in the darkness. This is called the **crayon resist technique.**

Paste together a landscape or cityscape using only colored construction paper. You may tear or cut the edges, but fill the entire page with collage. Will it be better to put the background or foreground items down first? Why? Perhaps you can use an ink line in the work.

Other Suggestions

After sketching the large shapes with pencil, use watercolors to paint a landscape. Start with light values first (like sky and light green places). Then add

the darker values as you continue. Have a single center of interest (the most important part of the painting). What might this center be in a seascape? In a cityscape?

Use one of the techniques explained in the still life section and paint a picture of your house, or part of the building where you live.

Use tempera paint to create an imaginary landscape that you might find on the moon or another planet. Use colors that give a feeling of mystery and strangeness.

A student used watercolor and ink to paint an old house in his neighborhood.

Elaine de Kooning used loose and slashing brush strokes to capture the spirit and feeling of sports action. Basketball, *42" × 32" (107 × 81 cm), is in oil on board. You can use other media to paint frantic action.*

To Catch the Action

Did you ever take a photograph of a running animal or a jumping person, only to find that parts of the photograph were blurred? Why might this happen? How can you use this information in your painting?

A standing telephone pole is vertical and balanced. If it starts to fall, it will become a diagonal pole. If it keeps falling, it will become a horizontal pole and rest on the ground. The pole was in three positions. Which of the three expresses *action*? How can you use this idea in painting people in action?

Painters have often tried to express action. They have used active and flowing brush strokes. They have tilted compositions or subjects. They have shown subject matter that is full of action. They have used violent clashes of color. You can also show action with a sketchy and incomplete style or with active brush work. Painters in the Baroque period (1600s) used swirling design and strong value contrasts to express action. Can you think of any other ways to show action?

Sports are usually full of action, but it is hard to stop the action long enough to sketch or paint it. Many artists use photographs to stop the action so they can study the movements, stresses and contrasts of the athletes. Then they use their own colors and brush work to emphasize the action. They do not try to copy photographs. Which sports might show the most exciting action?

If you have a camera, use it to get photographs of sports figures in action. Use one of your photographs as an example for a tempera painting that expresses action. Remember, you are painting an action picture, not one of the individual people in various poses.

Using tempera paint applied with a large brush in hurried strokes, try to create an abstract painting (one with no recognizable objects) that communicates action. You might also use crayon and water-color. What colors will help you communicate your message?

Use pencil with sweeping motions to express the action of running animals or crowds of people rushing about. Apply watercolor washes with similar sweeping strokes to bring color and more movement to the work. Why is there no need for detail in this type of work?

Other Suggestions

Use an idea from literature (or from your memory) to create a painting with great action.

Use watercolor to paint a seascape or landscape that expresses the violent action of a storm.

Can you write the word "ACTION" with water-color and brush to express the feeling of the word?

Basketball players, fighting for the ball, were painted in tempera from a photograph that stopped the action.

In this rapidly-painted watercolor, the artist tries to express the speed and action of a knight racing on horseback. A hurried, incomplete feeling adds to that sense of movement.

Use your imagination to combine many objects in a complex arrangement of shapes and colors. Many small shapes are drawn with colored markers to make one large, interesting shape.

Using Your Imagination

All the things you have ever imagined or seen in books, movies, television or your environment are stored in your mind. Painting is a marvelous way to bring them back into focus. You can recall experiences or invent new ones. You can use basic information (books, pictures, dreams, for example) to think up new ideas. Stretching your imagination is a good experience and can provide excellent material for paintings.

When you cannot go to a certain place to see things, you might look in books and magazines. For example, you cannot sketch when you are under water. But you can study underwater plant and animal life by looking at movies, books, slides or charts. Compose your own underwater environment with various animals, plants and fish. Use a mixed media technique, combining many materials to add interest to the work.

Make up your own animals or combine the features of several to create something new and different.

Paint a group portrait of your family or friends from memory. Try to remember how they look but don't worry about details. What environment might be used for such subjects?

Can you imagine life on another planet? How might other beings be shaped or colored? How might they travel and live? Use tempera paint to create a painting of life on another planet.

You can create imaginative artwork of familiar objects (insects, birds, animals). Watercolor and ink combine to produce this colorful butterfly.

This is an imaginary family portrait as remembered by a young artist. Figures and faces are concepts rather than actual likenesses in this tempera painting.

Other Suggestions

Use crayon, ink and watercolor to create a mixed media painting of life in the circus.

Use a scene from around your house for subject matter. Create your own color combinations and textures. Try to express your feeling about the subject.

Use mixed media to paint the face of an imaginary clown or animal. Provide a suitable background to fill the negative space.

Imagine scenes composed only of candy, or sports being played by people with four arms or musicians with wild musical instruments. Can you imagine other subjects that stretch your imagination and that of the viewer?

Create a combination painting, using magazine pictures and tempera paint. Glue the pictures or parts of pictures down first. Use color and paint to unify the work. You may want to use a single idea to unify the painting.

Glue string over the outline of a boat, portrait or animal design. Paint the picture with tempera. Use cardboard for the base of this relief painting. Can other relief items be added to your collage to add surface interest?

Cut a stencil of an animal, person or flower out of tagboard or other heavy paper. Use the stencils in several ways. Trace them on a sheet of paper with

You can use imagination in both subject matter (top) and technique (below). Tempera was used in both paintings, but the dream image combines collage with paint. The simple colors and shapes and the strong black outline give a familiar item a new look.

crayon or pencil. Use a stiff brush and tempera paint to stencil the image onto paper. Spatter thinned-out tempera with an old toothbrush through the stencil. Let the figures overlap. Design a full page using some or all of these methods. Fill in the background using tempera or crayon. Outline with crayon or pen and ink, if you think it is needed.

A very strange bird was created in a collage with scraps of paper. The paper was crayon-rubbed on textured surfaces and then covered with contrasting watercolor washes.

You can use a stencil knife to cut a black construction paper design. Give colored tissue paper or cellophane in place to produce a stained glass effect.

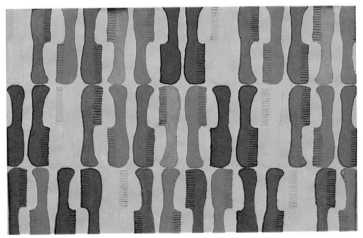

A simple shape (such as this comb) was repeated to form a fascinating surface pattern. Can you simplify other objects to create similar patterns?

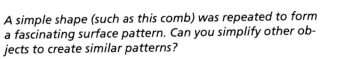

What's New in Painting?

Styles of painting are constantly changing. What is new today might well be out of style next year. A few ideas from the style of recent years will make you aware of what is happening in contemporary art. Look back at the section on contemporary art in this book. Review Hard Edge Painting, Pop Art and Op Art. Does this give you any ideas for your own work?

Nanci B. Closson paints in a variety of styles and techniques. In her acrylic work Green Rivers, *64" × 50" (162 × 128 cm), Closson explores the fluid quality of paint on unprimed canvas. Does this give you ideas for working with watercolor or thinned tempera paint?*

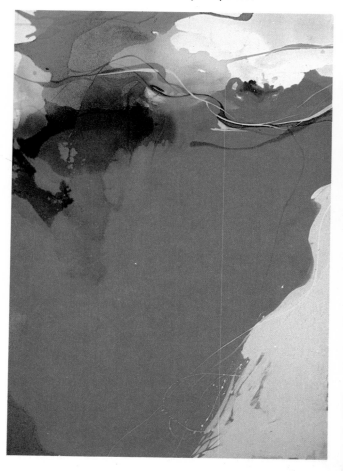

Op art designs can take many forms. These two will help you start. Change the sizes and spaces to produce visual excitement. If you can solve the spacing pattern in each of these, you can create many designs, as did these two students.

Wayne Thiebaud painted Jawbreaker Machine *in oil, 26" × 32" (66 × 81 cm). You may paint another machine or a common object in tempera or watercolor. William Rockhill Nelson Gallery of Art, Kansas City, Missouri.*

Robert Cottingham paints Super Realistic works, often using street signs and storefronts as subjects. J.C. *is acrylic on canvas, 21" × 23" (53 × 58 cm). For such careful and detailed work, it is necessary to "sketch" and gather information using a camera.*

Carla Pagliaro experiments by painting her canvas and then shaping it to form a wall sculpture. In this 84″ × 44″ × 13″ (214 × 112 × 33 cm) work, she also included wood in several places.

Do You Like to Experiment?

Experiments in painting might mean using traditional materials (watercolor, crayon, glue) in exciting combinations. But you can also experiment with painting surfaces, such as folded paper, glass, collaged panels, wood or cardboard. You may even make your own paint. Use powdered tempera, for example, mixed with things such as white glue, detergent, lacquer, powdered skim milk in a thick mixture or any sticky substance.

Can you think of ways to combine string, glue and tempera? Could you devise a way to include toothpicks in a painting?

These pages show examples of experimental painting techniques. Do they give you ideas for your own experiments?

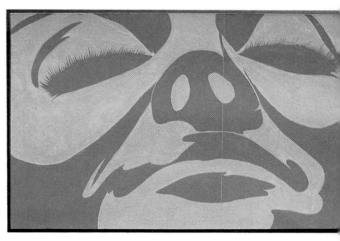

Using a small card with a 1″ × 2″ (2.5 × 5 cm) cutout opening, this student used part of a face from a magazine for subject matter. The image was greatly enlarged and simplified, and then painted in two solid colors with tempera paint.

Chuck Close is well known for his huge painted portraits. He also works with collage techniques. In Georgia, he used various values of flattened, gray, pulp paper blobs. He glued these to canvas to make this 48" × 38" (122 × 97 cm) image. Courtesy The Pace Gallery, New York.

Try changing your painting surface. A student made this box from cardboard and put the portrait inside the box.

Painting whole bottles is interesting, but a broken bottle can be more challenging. This is a watercolor painting.

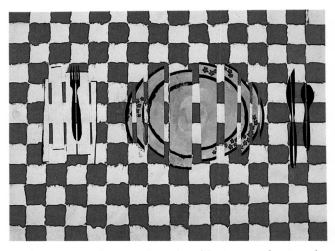

The student works here are examples of experimental painting. The still life above is a collage. Colored tissue paper was adhered to illustration board with clear lacquer.

In the Pop Art place setting, the objects were fractured, then rearranged and placed on a checkered table cloth.

In this combine painting, the young artist created a unique arrangement with a real plastic knife, some orange slices cut from a magazine and tempera paint.

String provides a strong outline for this tempera painting. The artist used an almost-dry brush (called dry brush
painting) to emphasize the relief features of the painting.

The two-foot long sneaker is cut out of wood and
painted. You could also use Masonite or cardboard. A
pop-top tab is tacked on the back for a hanger.

11 Printmaking

If you press your finger on an ink pad, and then on a sheet of paper, you have produced a print—a fingerprint. You can repeat the same print over and over again. You can reproduce the first image many times. That is what printmaking is all about.

Since each image is made from the original finger (or block, screen or carving), the prints are called *multiple originals*. Each print signed by the artist (no matter how many are made) is considered an original print.

The entire printmaking process is exciting: drawing and carving the design, inking the block, adding the paper and applying the pressure. Finally, the long-awaited print is pulled from the original block or plate and the first impression is finished. Then another. And another. And another, until the *edition* (total number of prints) is completed.

The Japanese printmaker Hiroshige (nineteenth century) and the German master Albrecht Dürer (sixteenth century) followed the same process. For several hundred years, printmaking techniques changed little. Etchings, woodcuts and, later, lithographs were produced in the same fashion. But today's printmaking is one of the most experimental areas of art. New materials (plastics, epoxies, resins) and newly devel-

oped inks, paints and paper, have given printmaking a new position of importance. People have begun to appreciate printmaking more and more. Now some galleries show only contemporary prints.

The processes involved in printmaking are fascinating. All prints are produced after a printing surface has been prepared with tools and materials. You might expect better prints after some practice with these tools. Woodcuts are carved with knives. Etching plates are scratched and engraved with tools and then eaten away with acid. Lithographic stones are marked with special crayons and inks. Silk-screen printing requires frames, stencils and squeegees. Other processes involve cutting, gluing, scraping, building up and using glass, wood, metal and various tools.

Several terms used in connection with producing multiple images should be understood. *Original prints* are made by the artist, and are called *impressions*. *Reproductions* are produced mechanically with cameras and printing presses; these are called *copies*. *Lithographic prints* and *posters* are also produced mechanically and are not considered original impressions, even if signed by the artists.

LeRoy Neiman has developed silk-screen prints (serigraphs) as an exciting means of expression. His prints move with splashes of color that vividly express sports action.

Andō Hiroshige was one of the nineteenth century master printmakers of Japan. He produced this multicolored woodcut, View of Nihomdashi. He supervised the work, but other craftspeople did most of the carving and actual printing, according to traditional Oriental work methods. Collection of Joseph Gatto.

175

Looking for Subject Matter

Because of the time and effort involved in preparing the printing surface, you should choose subjects that are important and interesting. After deciding *what* to print, make sketches to help you decide *how* to make your point. Which techniques and style will best express your ideas? Printmaking is an effective way to communicate ideas. Your technique should add to and carry out your idea.

Subjects might include horses, people, faces, landscapes, animals or still lifes; depression, joy or sorrow; geometric or repeated designs. The examples on these pages should help you think of others.

While subject matter is unlimited, each printmaking technique does have certain limitations. For example, it is difficult to produce fine detail in woodcut or linoleum prints. Etchings must make use of fine lines, not big flat areas. Mixing colors is easier in silk screen printing than in etching.

As you work with and look at examples of each material, you will learn to recognize its strengths and weaknesses. Which printmaking technique would you use to express delicacy, strength, summer, sorrow, spring or an elephant? Emphasize the best qualities of each material; do not push any technique beyond its capabilities.

A classroom plant was used as the subject of a white glue print (top). Glue was put on cardboard, and the cardboard was inked and printed with a press. The musician friends of the student artist are featured in the linoleum print.

Veloy Vigil printed his favorite horse subjects over a colored background. In Song of Pony, 22" × 15" (56 × 38 cm), the artist used traditional woodcut techniques in an unusual way.

A strong visual impact is created in this woodcut entitled Guitar Player *by Don LaViere Turner. Notice the variety of textures he developed. He used drills, nails, knives and gouges. Look for the contrast he achieves between solid black areas and the textured passages.*

Design Suggestions

In all printmaking, preparing the printing surface is very important. Work out your ideas first on paper. Then apply your ideas to the wood, linoleum, plastic or silk. Do not rush the carving, cutting or stencil making. Your satisfaction with the final print will depend on how carefully you prepare the printing surface. Remember that the print is actually a *reflection* of the prepared surface.

Look back to the section on design to recall the elements and principles that help produce good artwork. Ask yourself design questions. What kind of line will be best to use here? Do I have enough variety of texture to make the print interesting? Would more contrast between plain and textured areas add interest to my work?

String prints can create a combination of fine lines and flat shapes. Different kinds of string yield different types of lines. Soft brayers allow more ink on the background surface.

A single linoleum cut can produce many different designs. Here, the block was printed again and again over previous printings, using several colors of ink.

These student linoleum cuts and woodcuts show the characteristic feel of relief prints. Each print has strong contrasts, a rugged appearance and simplicity of shape and line.

Relief Prints

The very first relief prints were **woodcuts** that were simply outlines, often colored by hand. As time went by, these became more complicated, especially under the pen and knife of the German, Albrecht Dürer.

Any surface that has texture or raised areas can be inked and printed: auto tires, tree bark, shoe soles, radiator grills, your foot or a leaf. Can you think of other surfaces with texture? It might not be practical to ink some surfaces, but others can produce exciting printed images.

You can print from surfaces that you find. Or you can prepare flat surfaces for printing by cutting them or gluing things on. You might use regular printing ink or tempera paint applied with a brayer (a roller-applicator) or brush. You can print on bond paper, newspaper, construction paper, printing papers, rice paper or oatmeal paper. Try different papers to see what works best.

Any inked relief surface gives a mirror image when printed. This means it is a reverse image of the surface from which it is made.

To get used to the printing techniques, gather a box of wood scraps, roll printing ink on them and print the textures of the wood. Ink lightly and carefully to allow the grain of the wood to show. Use several on the same sheet of paper to make a design. Overlap them. Try several colors of printing ink.

You can buy prepared blocks of linoleum or a roll of unmounted battleship linoleum can be cut to any size and shape you want. Wood for making woodcuts should be soft to work well. The best wood is a piece of white pine. Tools for cutting wood or linoleum include V-shaped and U-shaped gouges and flat knives.

Try inking and printing wood scraps singly or in combinations. Get used to the process. Try several colors. Spoon-rubbing supplied pressure for these prints.

Pull the print from a linoleum cut and understand the concept of a mirror image. You get the subject that you carved, but reversed—like looking in a mirror.

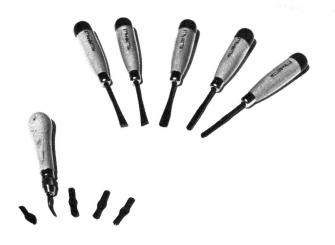

(A)

(C)

(B)

(D)

Woodcutting and linoleum cutting tools (A) include knives and several kinds of gouges. As you cut a linoleum block (B), push tools away from your body and hands. Here, a wood device holds the block still. Use brayers (C) to roll ink evenly on a flat plate (glass or similar). Use the brayer to put ink on your wood or linoleum block. Apply pressure to create the print. You can apply pressure with (D) a wooden spoon, a smooth stone, a baren or a press.

Other textural effects in wood can be made with sandpaper, pipe, nails, drills, screen or gravel pounded with a hammer. You also need brayers to apply the ink and an ink slab (glass, formica or metal sheet) on which to roll out the ink.

Try a few cuts on a sample of wood or linoleum to get the feel and action of the tools and knives. **Always cut away from you when using the gouges. Use all tools carefully.** Cut shallow areas of lines. They will print just as well as deep ones.

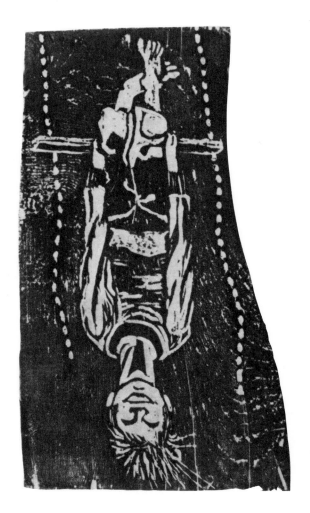

The artist cut two separate surfaces to print this two-color impression of musical instruments. The underlying color was made with a few simple shapes cut from the back of the plank of wood. On the front, the musical instruments were drawn, cut out and inked. This image was printed over the first color.

An irregular chunk of wood was the starting point for this print of a child swinging upside down. The student mixed the ink to get a neutral color.

Choose a subject that will work well on linoleum or wood block and make a few sketches. Then transfer your design to the block, but remember, it will print the reverse of the cut block. If words or letters are used, they must be cut backwards. Carbon paper or a soft pencil rubbed on the back of the drawing will help in the transfer. Blacken the areas to be printed on the block (wood or linoleum) with India ink or a black marker. This will make cutting the block less confusing. *White areas are the ones that get cut out*.

Begin cutting with either a knife or small V-shaped gouge, outlining the white areas. Be flexible in your cutting, ready to change the design.

Roll out ink on a glass sheet with your brayer. Ink should be evenly distributed on glass *and* brayer. Ink the block and place the paper on top. Apply pressure by rubbing with the bowl part of a large wooden spoon, or run the block and paper through a press. You might think of other ways to apply pressure.

Other Suggestions

Experiment with papers of various types, colors and textures.

Experiment with colored printing inks.

Roll a brayer full of ink on paper and use this as a background for your print. How else could you make prepared backgrounds?

Print with dark ink over a light print. Position the images upside down, reversed, or slightly overlapping.

You may print greeting cards, illustrations for newspapers, wrapping paper, monograms, calandar illustrations, notebook covers, prints for framing or cartoons. Can you think of other uses for prints?

Roughly-cut surfaces provide textural patterns for backgrounds in these two linocuts. The large, simple, positive shapes were detailed with thin line cuts.

String, laid on a bead of white glue, is the simple material for a string print.

Cardboard letters are cut from tag board and glued to a cardboard backing. They are rolled carefully with a brayer and printed. Remember, glue the letters and words *backwards* to have them correct on the print.

More Relief Prints

Linoleum cuts and woodcuts are the usual relief printing methods. But any relief surface (one with raised areas) that ink will stick to can be printed. Perhaps one or more of the projects on these pages will appeal to you. Or you might invent new ways to develop a printable relief surface.

String prints are made by making a line drawing on heavy cardboard and gluing string over the line. Put a bead of white glue on the line and lay string onto it. A toothpick might help position the string in the right place. A coat of shellac will seal the surface and make the inking easier. Roll ink on the surface with a soft brayer, put the paper on top and apply pressure with a *soft* brayer or a press. Interesting variations can be made by running a partly inked brayer (blot it first on a sheet of newspaper) over the paper that is placed on the string design. Does this give you any other ideas for printing?

Cardboard prints (tagboard, thin folio board or even heavy paper) can be made by cutting the cardboard into letters or shapes with scissors or knives. Glue these to a rigid surface (such as heavy folio board). Try to keep the raised areas the same thickness. Give the entire surface a coat of shellac. This will stop the ink from soaking into the material. Then ink and print. Remember that the letters and the designs will be reversed when printed.

Other Suggestions

String prints can be made quite large. Perhaps you would like to produce a full-size portrait of yourself. What materials could you use for a backing board?

Print string designs on colored tissue papers and later collage them (either whole or torn) onto white cardboard. Experiment by putting several layers on top of each other.

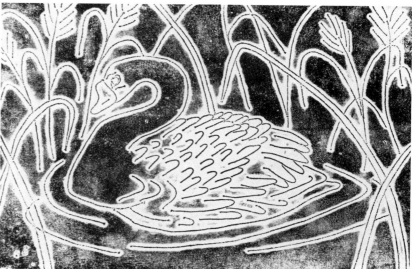

These two string prints began in the same way but were printed differently. The swan was inked and printed in a press. A sheet of clean paper was placed over the plate of the dancing girl, and a soft, inked brayer was rolled over the surface.

This prowling tiger print combines relief techniques using cardboard, string and glue. Can you see where each was used?

185

For this subtractive monoprint, the artist smeared and removed ink with fingers, a crumpled piece of paper and a brush handle. Could you use this technique to produce a landscape or portrait print?

This additive monoprint was made by lightly pouring and dripping tempera paint on a glass plate. Paper was laid over it and hand-rubbed lightly.

Monoprints

While other printmaking techniques allow for the production of many duplicate images, monoprinting produces only one. However, there are several ways to produce monoprints.

In the **subtractive method**, an even coat of ink or tempera paint is rolled on a sheet of glass, plastic or formica. Here is a beautiful surface on which to experiment. Use brushes, sticks, fingers, paper scraps or nails to remove ink and create a design on the surface. Place a sheet of paper (either damp or dry) over the surface and apply pressure with a brayer or press. Then pull up the print.

In the **additive method**, you apply colored printing inks or tempera paints with brushes, fingers or paper to a glass surface or plastic sheet. Pour, drip, smear and smudge until you like the mixture of colors and textures. Lay paper over the surface and apply pressure with your hand, a spoon, a brayer or a press. Then pull up the print.

The **lift method** involves more drawing. *Evenly* ink a glass sheet with a brayer. Blot the sheet lightly with a piece of newspaper to remove excess ink. Lay a clean sheet of paper over the inked plate and draw on the paper with a sharp pencil, crayon or ball-point pen. The ink will transfer to the front side of the paper. Shading can be accomplished by rubbing lightly with your fingers or the palm of your hand. The drawing can be created right at the time or it can be drawn on the paper before printing. If more colors are desired, re-ink the plate for each color and repeat the process. Keep the drawing simple.

Other Suggestions

Edges of prints can be kept even and clean by making a two- or three-inch mat of tagboard or heavy paper with an opening the size you want to print. Lay this on the plate after inking and then place the paper to be printed over it.

Martin Green's huge monoprint, Mountainside, *81" × 43" (204 × 107 cm) was pulled from four plates. The original design was painted on the plates. Which of the three monoprint techniques did the artist use? Louis Newman Galleries, Beverly Hills.*

If several colors are to be printed, you might use registration marks to get your paper back in the same place each time. Or you can simply tape the top edge of your printing paper to the glass, and raise and lower it between printings.

Print on colored paper, wallpaper, textured or smooth papers. Or print on tissue paper, cloth or on paper that has been painted first. Can you think of other prepared surfaces on which to print?

Thin or thick papers have advantages in each method. Try some to see what works best for you.

If inks dry too much before printing, spray *lightly* with water or use dampened paper for the print. You can add glycerin to the inks or paints *before* rolling them on the glass. This will slow the drying time.

Make abstract prints by emphasizing textures, line or color, without introducing recognizable subject matter.

This simple line drawing and more complex shaded study both are lift-method monoprints. Gray areas are made by rubbing very lightly with fingers.

Make a stencil monoprint by inking a plate and laying objects on it. Here, leaves and grass were used. Put paper on top. Apply pressure by hand. What other stencils might be fun to use?

Experimental Prints

There are many experimental printing techniques that artists and designers are exploring. Most of them work with the relief features of objects or plates. Here are some suggestions that might challenge your imagination.

Leaves, twigs, pressed flowers and grasses can be flattened, then glued lightly to a backing and printed. What printing techniques might be used to make such nature prints? Make balanced arrangements interesting by using a wide range of materials.

If you have sheets of sandpaper, you might make drawings on them with a wax crayon. Ink the drawing with a soft brayer. Apply pressure for the print with a press or a brayer.

Rubber erasers can be cut into small designs, inked from an inked pad and printed. How else could these techniques by used?

Potatoes or turnips can be cut and printed with tempera paint to make designs.

White glue can be trailed on a glass sheet or piece of masonite, allowed to dry, inked and printed with a brayer.

Felt, burlap and other textured scraps of textiles can be arranged on a backing, glued down, inked and printed.

Automobile tire tubes or pieces of neoprene can be cut into interesting shapes with scissors, glued to a backing and printed.

Burlap and other textured cloth pieces were cut and glued to cardboard, then inked and printed.

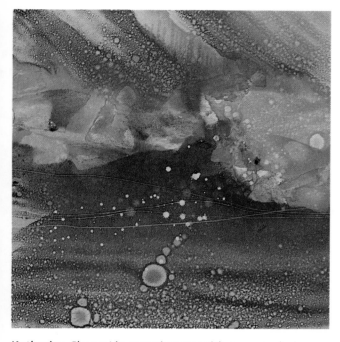

Katherine Chang Liu experiments with many techniques to create monoprints. Hers are colorful, personal and exciting. Louis Newman Galleries, Beverly Hills.

This channel print was made by folding a sheet of paper, opening it, adding blobs and drips of tempera, closing and rubbing gently by hand. The possibilities are endless.

12 Sculpture

The Italian sculptor Michelangelo stood before a huge chunk of marble much larger than himself. In one hand he grasped a saw-toothed chisel; in the other a wooden mallet. At his feet were dozens of sheets of drawings and scribbles. He looked again at the solid form of white marble, trying to visualize a human form inside. His aim was to release that form from its rocky prison. He laid his chisel against the cold stone and began to pound with the heavy mallet.

In Michelangelo's time (sixteenth century) most sculptors worked in much the same way, carving the form of a person from a block of stone. After all, sculptors had been working this way for thousands of years. Other sculptors cast liquid metal into human or animal forms; some carved in wood. When they were finished, you could walk around their work and look at it from any side. It was three-dimensional.

Today, a sculptor's studio might contain welding torches, fiberglass, cans of epoxy glue, sheets of steel, saws, pliers, wood, metal, fiber or textiles. Artists can be polishing aluminum, using chain saws to cut huge logs, experimenting with great factory machinery, cutting glass, pouring resins, arranging electrical parts or using the ancient techniques of bronze casting or marble sculpture.

A sculpture is three-dimensional, having height, width and depth, while a painting is usually two-dimensional, having only height and width. Some sculptures might be mounted against a wall (relief sculpture) but they will still be three-dimensional.

How does sculpture differ from painting? From how many sides can a drawing be seen? Why is sculpture sometimes called "art in the round"?

Not all sculpture is huge. Can you think of very small sculptural works? Are there any sculptures in your town or at your school? Can you remember seeing any sculptures on your vacations? Have you seen pictures of sculptures in this country or other countries around the world?

Start a collection of magazine pictures that show different types of sculpture in various materials. What type of presentation can you prepare?

Hold a stream-worn pebble in your hand. Feel its smoothness, texture and form. A craggy chip of stone has been tumbled by the stream into a smooth round form. Changing an original form to produce another, more desirable form is sculpture.

Greek, Roman and Renaissance sculptors were interested in volume and mass. They tried to arrange solid forms in functional and interesting ways. Today's sculptors are just as interested in the holes and

In 1501, Michelanglo sculpted his Pieta (Mary weeping over her dead son). He used a single block of white marble. The piece is larger than life-size, highly polished, and beautifully crafted in every detail. Note especially the details in flesh and cloth. This sculpture is in a chapel of St. Peter's Basilica, Rome.

Kent Ullberg designed Wind in the Sails. He made it to stand near the Gulf of Mexico in Corpus Christi, Texas. This sculpture is made of polished stainless steel. It is mounted on a red granite base and is 23½' (7 meters). The work was formed in clay and cast in stainless steel. See the artist at work on page 198.

David Smith's Cubi XXIII *is welded stainless steel, 76" × 172" (193 × 437 cm). In this sculpture the polish marks are a planned part of the surface texture. Notice the variety of materials and styles in the work on this page. Los Angeles County Museum of Art, Contemporary Art Council Fund.*

open spaces. They want to lead your eye *into* and *around* the objects, inviting you to explore the contours and the three-dimensions of their creations.

Sculpture invites you to *feel* as well as to see, even though signs warn you "Do Not Touch!" When working on your own sculpture, your hands *feel* the surfaces as they form, bend or explore the form you are creating. Smooth, coarse, gritty, lumpy, soft, solid, open, wiry or grainy surfaces can be felt. Both surface textures and the entire form of the sculpture can be experienced with your hands as well as your eyes.

Sculptures have been used to show impressions or feelings (such as the *Statue of Liberty*, *The Thinker* by Rodin, or an heroic statue in a city park). They can be religious, funny, patriotic, inspiring, public, personal, tragic or exciting. A sculpture may be the main feature in a city plaza. It may be placed on top of your television set. Sculpture can show animals, hu-

Betty Davenport Ford designs animals in a very personal style. African Porcupine *is an 18" (46 cm) long ceramic sculpture. It emphasizes a textured surface and stylized form. Courtesy the artist and Dalzell Hatfield Galleries, Los Angeles.*

mans or abstract forms, alone or in combinations. re-gardless of the purpose, technique, material or size, sculpture is a three-dimensional art form.

How do you begin working on a three-dimensional project? Glance over this chapter to get an idea of the directions you might take. Check on available materials: wood blocks, toothpicks, reeds; clay, glazes, kilns; scraps, glue, paints; sandpaper, files, saws, nails; wire, paper, cardboard, plaster; buckets, dishes, newspapers. You may be familiar with some of the materials, others may take some practice be-fore you feel comfortable with them.

Auguste Rodin's sculptures were usually hand-formed from clay, then cast in bronze. The Thinker *reveals Rodin's finger- and hand-prints in the finished work. The National Gallery of Art, Washington D.C. (gift of Mrs. John W. Simpson).*

Isamu Noguchi sculpted For the Issei *from Japanese red granite. The two huge blocks of stone are partly in their natural form and partly carved by the artist. This is an Oriental sculptural concept. The work is in the Little Tokyo area of Los Angeles.*

Design Suggestions

You should learn to *think* in three dimensions. You must consider all viewing angles and sides, not just a front view. Turn the sculpture as you work, to give all sides equal attention.

You may begin by making sketches of *general* shapes and deciding on textural details. But remember that all sides are to be sculpted. You may begin by holding a lump of clay, modeling it and shaping it into a face. You may start with a single toothpick and add to it to create your structure. After working in

Lou Rankin used cement, sand, steel nails and glass marbles to create Owl. *The artist enjoys experimenting and combining many materials to create sculptures of animals and birds. This one emphasizes form and texture.*

three-dimensions on a project or two, the ideas of form and space, of mass and volume, of three-dimensions will mean something to you.

What would you like to sculpt? If you would like to create a cat, you must think about which materials would be best to use. You might want to work with plaster. You may work on a project where you experiment with materials and don't produce a likeness of any living thing. Animals (real or imaginary), people, plants, birds, bugs, imaginary forms, nonobjective (abstract) forms can all be created. Select methods and materials that will fit your project. Would clay be a wise choice for making a spindly-legged colt? Would toothpicks be a good material for making an elephant?

As you work on your sculpture, look back at the section of this book that discusses the elements and principles of design (line, shape, space, color, value, texture; balance, unity, contrast, pattern, movement, rhythm). Remember these elements and principles as you work on your sculptures.

Regardless of subject matter and materials, a basic work plan can be followed.

1. Decide on your subject matter. Look through this book and others to help you select. Your library or a museum might be helpful. See what others have done. Make some sketches to get started.
2. Determine the best materials to use. Gather them together. You may have worked with some materials before; others may be new to you. Do you want to experiment? Would you rather try to improve your techniques with a familiar material?
3. Decide which techniques will work best. Will carving, modeling or constructing work best with your material? Notice how other students or artists have handled the problems of subject, materials and techniques.
4. Begin the sculpture.

Keep your first projects simple. Work on all sides of the sculpture as you go. Notice the interacting movements and forms as the work proceeds. Any decoration should fit comfortably with the form, looking like it belongs. Consider textures, colors and finishes as you work. Make good craftsmanship an important goal.

Kent Ullberg's dramatic sculpture of playful otters is called Ring of Bright Water. The 25" (64 cm) high work is polished stainless steel. It emphasizes movement, rhythm, form and concept.

Here students enjoy Claes Oldenberg's sculpture, Giant Three-Way Plug. The artist has enlarged a common object to gigantic proportions. The piece is made of wood and plywood, and is 58" (141 cm) high.

195

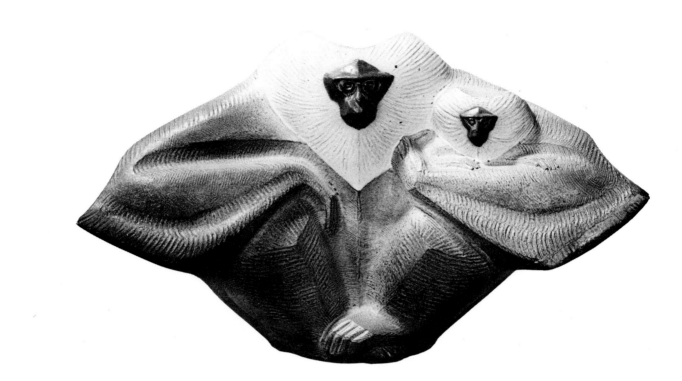

This delicate porcelain work was created by Elena Canavier, who uses clay to make personal statements about the sea. Tide Pool Bowl *is 8" (20 cm). It is part of a continuing series of crafted pieces that bear the artist's distinctive glazes.*

Betty Davenport Ford is a master of style and form. Her Mother and Baby Marmosette Monkey *is 17" (43 cm) high. She modeled it of ceramic clay. Then she carved, textured, glazed and fired it. Courtesy of the Dalzell Hatfield Gallery, Los Angeles.*

Modeling

Working with your hands to form and shape a material is what modeling is all about. Clay is the major modeling material. It is also one of the oldest materials used to shape and form things. Papier-mâché is another material used for modeling.

Modeling can be an exciting and personal art form. You can create objects using only your own hands. As you handle the materials, it may seem that the object expresses what *you* feel—perhaps more than any other art form.

Clay

Whether you work with plasticine (an oil-based clay) or wet clay (the kind that can be fired), you are sculpting with earth. Clay comes from the ground and is mixed with other earth materials that make it both workable and able to hold its shape. You might find clay in your neighborhood. But for most of us, clay comes in plastic bags, ready to use.

What tools can be used to work with clay? Would you consider your hands as sculpting tools? In modeling, your hands are the most important tools. Read the discussion on ceramics in the crafts section of this book to help you understand the process, techniques and tools.

Plasticine is an oil-based clay that softens with the warmth of your hands and is easily formed with your fingers. Pieces can be squeezed off or stuck on. Large pieces get quite heavy and wire or wood frameworks are often needed to keep the form from sagging. This clay comes in colors that might help you get ideas for decorating. However, finished work in plasticine cannot be fired or glazed.

Wet clay ranges from low-fire clay to high-fire stoneware. It comes in several colors and textures. If a kiln is available, you might consider working with clay that can be fired. Adding grog (ground firebrick) to the clay will give better drying, a stronger sculptural structure and an interesting texture.

Cover ceramic sculptures with plastic when you are not working on them. This keeps them moist and workable. Wet clay sculptures should be hollow if they are more than an inch thick in any place. This allows drying and prevents explosions in the firing process.

Sculptures can be formed around one or more pinch pots (see the ceramics section) or by the coil or slab methods. Decorations can be stamped or scratched into the surface with sticks, buttons, plastic

This clay face, displaying emotion, is the work of a junior high student.

pieces or other tools. Glazing sometimes adds to the sculpture, but often covers up fine decoration. Add color only if it will improve the final work. Stains often work better on sculptures than glazes.

Invent an animal sculpture, starting with two pinch pots about as big as your fist. Add a head, legs or other features. Decorate it by stamping, piercing or adding to it. To add parts, scratch the surfaces to be joined and add slip (liquid clay) before joining them. Smooth the joints as you model the clay. Try to stylize the features and forms rather than attempt a realistic copy of an animal. Think of a variety of textures as you decorate. Bisque fire and then stain or glaze.

You may use plasticine for the same type of sculpture. But start with solid pieces instead of pinch pots.

197

Slabs of clay make the sides of this house. The windows, roof and details were scratched and carved from the slabs. Glazes add color.

Kent Ullberg is working on a huge clay model for his 23' (7 m) high work. It is to be cast in stainless steel. A skeleton of wood and steel supports the massive weight while the artist works.

You may make a single pinch pot as big as a baseball and use it as the start of a clown's head. Add features and decorations and mold them with your hands to exaggerated proportions. You may use this technique to produce other faces with exaggerated features. What coloring might add to your sculpture?

Other Suggestions

Make a clay ice cream sundae, a shoe, a purse or other piece of clothing or food. Glaze or color the fired piece with bright acrylic paint. Can you think of other things that might make interesting ceramic pieces in this Pop Art technique.

Bisqueware can be stained with thinned acrylic paint by brushing on and rubbing off again. Several transparent layers might produce interesting surfaces.

Check in the ceramics section of this book for other ideas for decorating or finishing your sculpture.

This ceramic fish was carved (rather than formed) from a solid piece of clay, about 1' (30 cm) long. It was hollowed out before firing to prevent an explosion in the kiln.

An eighth grade student created this papier-mâché buffalo using the strip method.

Papier-Mâché

The French term *papier-mâché* is used for several methods of work, all involving liquid paste and newspaper. Sculptures formed in this material can range from several inches to huge creations of ten feet or more. The inside structures can vary from wadded-up paper to a welded steel frame work.

There are three methods of working with papier-mâché.

For the **pulp method**, shred newspaper into thin strips or confetti-sized bits and soak in water for up to two days. Drain the water and add wheat paste until the material is like soft modeling clay. Wallpaper paste can also be used, a few drops of oil of clove will prevent spoilage. The pulp method is best for small sculptures. The pulp can be modeled like soft clay. Let the object dry completely and then decorate. Can you think of good subject matter for such sculptures?

For the **strip method**, tear newspaper into long strips about an inch wide. Dip the strips into wheat

A colorful display of students' papier-mâché puppets brightens up a seventh grade classroom.

paste (a creamy, thick mixture). Lay them in layers over the form until it is strong enough for your project. You may need five or six layers. The basic form can be wads of paper taped together, found objects (like boxes or plastic bottles), cardboard structures, wire wrapped with paper or cloth or a combination of these things.

For the **sheet method**, brush wallpaper (wheat) paste on a sheet of newspaper. Lay another sheet on top of it and smooth with the brush or your hand. Add a layer of paste and another sheet. Repeat for six or eight layers. When this has dried to a leathery sheet, cut and form it as you like. Allow it to harden. Paper tape or strips of soaked newspaper can seal cracks or joints. This method is excellent for producing drapery, large folds in cloth or abstract forms.

The ink used to print newspapers contains toxic chemicals and is petroleum based. Newsprint paper which has never been printed on is therefore recommended for use in making papier-mâché.

Looking at sculptures will give you ideas for your own. But perhaps some of these ideas will get you started.

Create an imaginative animal form by using found containers or cardboard shapes as a base (such as egg cartons, milk bottles, cereal cartons). Tape them together with masking tape. Use the strip method to coat the shape with enough layers of paper to make it strong. When dry, glue string with white glue to decorate the shape, and paint it with tempera colors. Finish with two coats of shellac.

Make a two-foot-high wire armature form of an active human form. Wrap torn strips of cloth around the wire to build up the form. Use the strip method to wrap paper around and finish the form. Decorate and shellac.

Create a hand puppet that is a character from one of your literature classes. Start with a Styrofoam ball (or other shape) and poke a hole for your finger. Add features using the pulp method. Imagine and create cartoon features. When dry, sand smooth and paint with tempera. Create a costume to fit your hand. Perhaps you and some classmates can dramatize a part of the character's story.

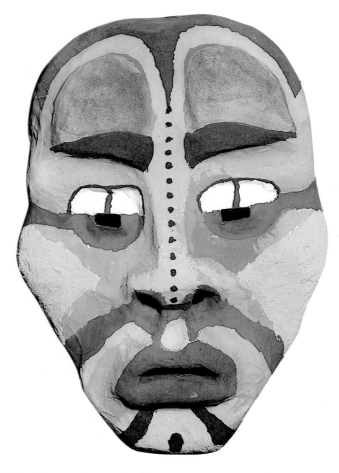

Primitive masks can inspire you to create a mask of your own. This one, painted with tempera by a seventh grade student, shows thoughtful use of color and symmetry.

A Mexican artist created this candle holder, using the sheet method to form the dress. Paint and several coats of lacquer produce a high gloss finish.

Red Grooms has developed papier-mâché into gigantic art forms. His pieces are often found in museums. This view shows only a small part of Ruckus Rodeo, a permanent installation at the Fort Worth Museum of Art. Viewers actually walk into the rodeo setting. They become part of the art experience.

Here a wire armature (inner support) was wrapped with paper and tape. It was covered with the strip method. This can produce long, thin figures.

Other Suggestions

Study the main features of primitive masks. Make a basic shape for a mask by forming cardboard, wadded-up paper, modeling clay, wire mesh or other materials. Use the pulp method (or simply soak facial tissues in wheat paste) to add details and features. Use the strip method to strengthen the surface. You can remove the basic shape underneath easily if you coat it with green soap or vaseline before applying the first papier-mâché. Decorate and shellac the mask.

Small features and details can be formed by dunking facial tissues in wheat paste, squeezing partially dry and sticking in place. Form the features with your fingers.

Groups of students might work together on large structures. Totem poles can be built around ice cream containers or cardboard poles (see a local carpet dealer). Faces go on both sides of totem poles. The paint should be bright and bold.

Constructing

Artists have carved and modeled sculpture for many centuries. But constructions have entered the art world only in recent years. Today, all types of materials are glued, nailed or welded, to produce three-dimensional forms. Many construction activities use materials that were not originally intended for sculpture, such as wire, nails, glass, plastic or paper. As you work on these projects, think of scraps from your garage or some workshop in town that you could use in constructions.

Wire

Outside of art activities, what is wire used for? Do any of these uses suggest sculpture ideas to you? Why can wire be called three-dimensional line?

Did you ever try to bend wire into shapes? Can wire be used to make an apple? A person? A dog?

Because of its linelike quality, artists have used wire to produce very simple to highly complicated sculptures. Some artists use soft wire, while others use wire that is thick and strong. Gold or silver wires are also used. Welders may use welding rods.

Select wire that bends easily but will not collapse. Heavy stovepipe wire or galvanized steel wire (both 18 gauge) work well, but many kinds of scraps are usable. Electrical wiring has a plastic coating that is very colorful to use. (Coat hangers are generally too difficult to bend.)

Cut a single piece of wire three feet long. Bend and twist it into a simple human figure. Start at the middle and form a small loop for the head. Then begin to work on the rest of the figure, twisting and shaping. You might need to use a pair of pliers, but most of the forming should be done with your fingers. After the basic figure (head, torso, arms and legs) has been formed, twist and bend the sculpture

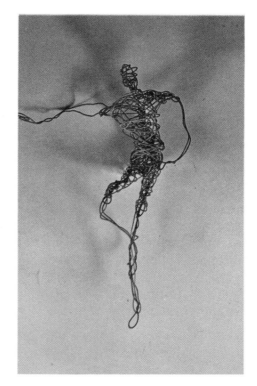

A student used soft, thin wire to produce this active figure. The wire is wrapped and balled up.

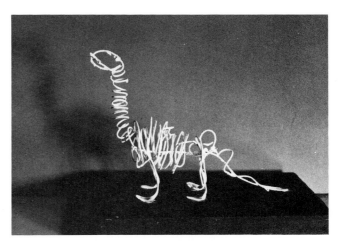

Coiled wire can make a simple but effective animal.

into a truly active, three-dimensional form. Turn it around and look at it from all angles. Either fix it to a base or form it to stand or sit by itself.

Construct several three-dimensional wire sculptures of human or animal forms, each from about three feet of wire. Keep forms simple and bend them into active forms. Combine them into a group sculpture and tie them together with thin wire. What group activities besides sports might work well for this purpose? Spread acrylic modeling paste or liquid metal (Sculpmetal) over the wire for more substance. **Read label instructions carefully before using either of these materials. Follow all safety precautions.** The entire sculpture can be spray painted, brushed with acrylic paint or left alone. **Use spray paint only in a room with active ventilation.**

Some sculptures use wire and a liquid such as Sculptmetal or acrylic modeling paste. These establish solid forms.

Other Suggestions

Cut and flatten aluminum cans. This metal can be trimmed and designed into shapes that can be added to wire sculptures.

Window screen or aluminum foil can be wired to the wire frame. Then acrylic modeling paste can be spread over the form to create a solid-looking sculpture.

Experiment with paints and inks for interesting finishes. You may apply acrylic paint (thinned with water), and while wet, rub part of it off for a shiny effect. What other colorings might be tried?

Bugs and insects make interesting subjects for wire sculptures.

Modeling paste and liquid metal can be sanded or filed to any degree of smoothness. Or they can be left alone with rough textures. **If you sand or file your sculpture, wear a respirator. Dust from these materials can harm your lungs.**

You might experiment using more wire to wrap a figure completely or partially. There are many things to try if you have time and a supply of different kinds of wires. Thin and supple wire, like that used by florists, or found in armatures from old motors, can be used to tie larger wires in place or to wrap around sculptures for a more solid form.

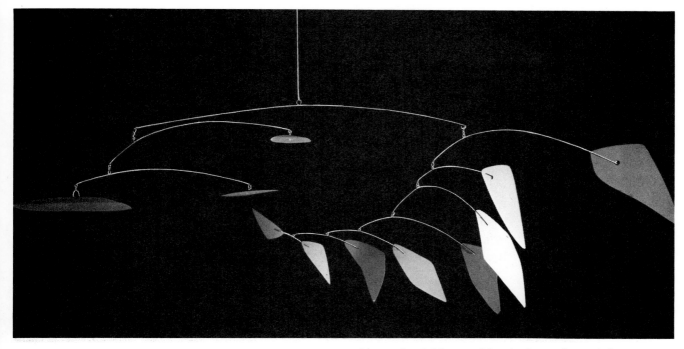

Alexander Calder combined wire and metal shapes to create Three Big Dots. The mobile has a span of 115" (297 cm). It is installed in the Baltimore Museum of Art.

A student used wire, aluminum trimmed from a soft drink can and liquid metal to create this praying mantis.

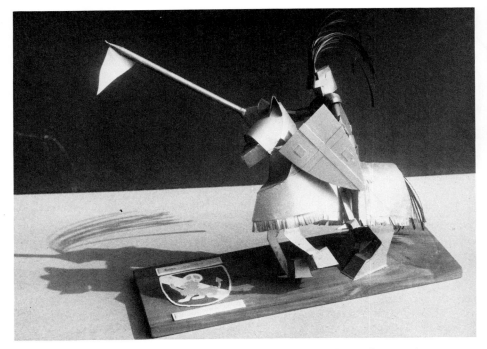

Paper is cut, rolled, scored and formed to produce an armored knight with lance on a charging steed.

Paper and Cardboard

Artists have used paper for hundreds of years. But it has always been as the surface for drawing, prints or paintings. Can paper be used for anything other than painting or drawing? Try folding or forming a single sheet of typing paper so it will support this art book. Does this suggest sculptural forms that might be created from paper?

Cardboard and paper are among our most common materials. A look in the trash can will reveal just how much we think of them—we throw away hundreds of pounds a year. Yet, both cardboard and paper can be exciting materials from which to create three-dimensional forms.

Use scraps of paper (drawing paper or throwaways from printing shops). Trim, cut, fold or form them into small, three-dimensional forms and glue them to a flat surface. Make many of the same forms. Create a structural surface pattern by gluing them in a repeated pattern to a heavy paper or cardboard backing. Notice the way light reflects on the pattern as

you turn it in various ways. Sculpture that projects from a wall or flat surface like this is called *relief sculpture* .

Other Suggestions

Experiment with ways of forming paper by bending, pleating, folding, cutting or scoring (making a partial cut with a razor blade or stencil knife to produce a sharp or curved fold; you can use an old ball-point pen for this also). Use some of these methods of forming paper to produce three-dimensional figures of faces, animals or people.

Huge abstract cardboard forms can be produced from parts of large carboard cartons. Cut them into irregular shapes (or geometric shapes), notch deeply and assemble your creation. Cut holes in the large sheets so you can see through the sculpture. Can you think of ways to use these forms as sculpture for your school, or in the set decoration for a play?

Books on paper sculpture (see lists in the back of this book) can supply dozens of ideas.

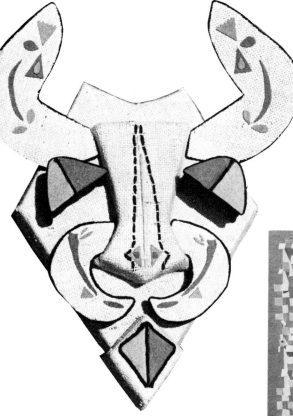

Cardboard was cut, scored, taped and formed to make the foundation for this mask. Fabric, yarn and colored cloth provide decoration.

These relief structures are formed of scraps and strips of paper, in a rhythmic pattern. Several ideas are shown, but hundreds can be created.

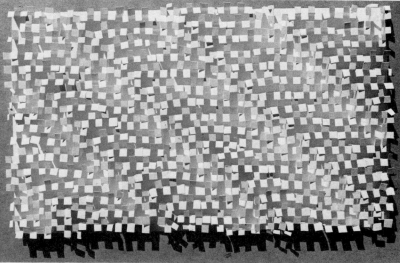

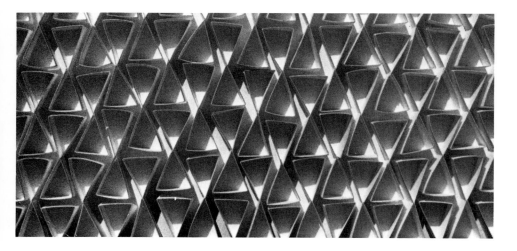

Wood Constructions

Wood is warm and responsive and can be used by artists in many ways. For centuries, the only sculptural use of wood was carving, but that has changed. Contemporary artists *construct* sculpture by adding piece to piece. Wood can be glued, nailed, tied, banded with metal strips or put together with wooden dowels. Wood is used for sculpture in the round or relief pieces that hang on walls. How might wood sculptures be finished? What features of wood give it an interesting surface?

Build a wooden structure, using toothpicks as a basic material. Glue the flat wood pieces first to a base of cardboard and begin your construction by adding pieces to it. Your form may be quite regular (using repeated units), or it may be free flowing and abstract. Use white glue or airplane glue. Reed or applicator sticks (thin dowels) can add interest and variety. Small toothpick structures can be dipped in plaster of paris for a different feeling.

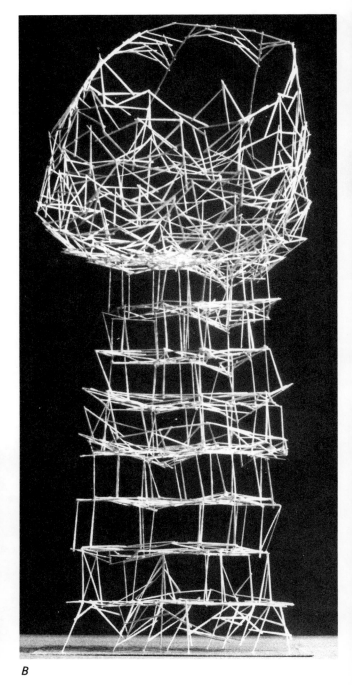

B

A

Toothpick structures can be freeform (A) or can have a more structured appearance (B). White glue holds these constructions in shape.

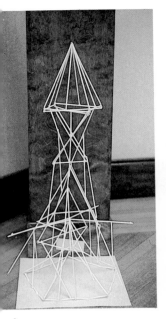

A   B   C

Student artists used toothpicks (B and C) and drinking straws (A). They created personal statements in three-dimensional line.

The coach is helping a young baseball player. This clever sculpture is made from balsa wood and applicator sticks. Does this make you think of other sculptural ideas?

Assemblages and More

Artists always search for new materials. They might use neon tubes, formed plastic, recording tapes, light bulbs, small computers, sheets of glass or mirrors, fur, hair, fabrics, a sewing machine or combinations of these.

Assemblages combine various materials into sculptural forms. Often these are found objects or manufactured items. But they can also be wood, metal or stone already worked on by the artist. There is no limit to the creative activities of sculptors today. This differs greatly from the days of Michelangelo and the Renaissance.

What other three-dimensional structures can you work with in your classroom? Some of the projects outlined here make use of familiar materials; others might spark new ideas.

Are there industrial products in your community that can be used in sculpture? Are there raw materials in your local environment? Several items that might inspire sculpture are stained glass, sawdust, bricks (wet and dry), lumber scraps, sheet metal, paper, plastics or fiberboard. Which local industries might have surplus items that you might use?

Put together scraps of wood and other objects to make people shapes, toys or funny animals. Or group scraps to produce an interesting abstract form. Paint the structure with bright colors, using tempera or acrylic paints.

What kind of construction could you build if you had a large supply of cardboard cartons? How could

it be decorated? Where might such a large construction be placed in your school?

Create masks by cutting, forming and taping cardboard pieces. Glue on cloth scraps of various textures and colors. What other found items can be glued on the surface to create decorative interest?

Put together a cube of cardboard and decorate each of the six sides with different textures or patterns. Use various materials, paints, found objects, cut scraps of cloth or paper to decorate.

Heavy string dipped in plaster can be wrapped around an inflated balloon, making a framework for the form. When dry, pop the balloon and hang the delicate form from a thin wire. How might these forms be decorated?

Wrap plaster-dipped strips of cloth around a wire framework to produce a strong, wiry figure. Decorate with paint and shellac.

Using a classmate or yourself as a model, cut facial features (eyes, nose, lips, head) from cardboard. Glue these to a heavy board cut in the shape of a head. Glue string to the surface to outline shapes or to produce line. Glue a sheet of aluminum foil over this and press firmly against the forms. Add thinned acrylic paint or India ink and partly rub away to produce a shine. This will emphasize highlights on this low-relief sculpture.

After you have glanced through this list, you might think of other assemblages. If you can get the materials, give it a try.

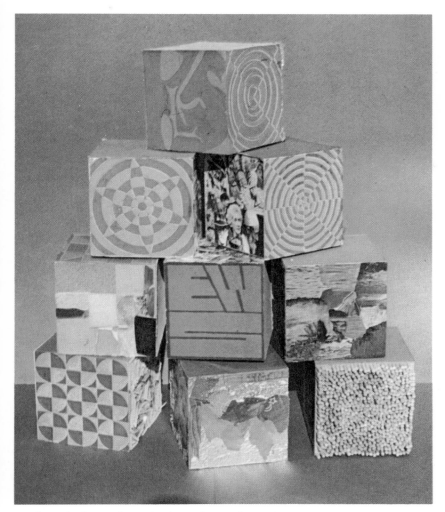

Students built cardboard cubes. The students then covered each side with different patterns, textures or both.

Hierarchy *is a construction designed to hang on a wall. Richard Wiegmann created it as a mixed-media construction of wood, cardboard, silk-screened parts and Ping-Pong balls.*

Found objects can be assembled in many ways. They can express new ideas and concepts.

13 Graphic Design

Graphic design is used for communication. Graphic designers combine symbols, images, words and colors. They use imaginative techniques to communicate ideas and information. Such artists work with a tremendous variety of styles, media and type. Their goal is to attract us and inform us about their clients' products and ideas.

Communication art may be found in books, magazines, annual reports, advertisements, television graphics, package designs, film previews and posters. Graphic designs may appear anyplace where businesses tell the public about themselves.

The Poster

Perhaps the most basic graphic design form is the poster. Posters have been used for centuries to advertise performances, products, services and other items that need public attention.

Look in your school, neighborhood and town. You will see posters on windows, walls and display cases. Posters are in and on buses and subway cars. Wherever people stand and wait, posters are likely to appear.

There are two-dimensional and three-dimensional posters. Designers sometimes use bright lights, moving parts, and even sound to add impact. Some posters have tall, vertical shapes. Others are horizontal.

Many posters are multicolored. Others use color sparingly for a different kind of dynamic treatment.

Posters are widely used to promote school and community activities. Through posters, students, teachers and parents learn about safety, health, human relations, school plays, dances, athletic events, club meetings and seasonal activities. During elections, students running for office use posters to try to earn your vote.

Properties of a Poster

1. A poster must catch the eye.
2. A poster must have a brief, direct message. (Posters are read by people on the move.)
3. A poster must be convincing. This is accomplished by combining letters, illustrations, symbols and color in the most effective way.
4. A poster should be simple. It should include only those things needed to make the message complete.

This colorful poster was designed to be seen in insurance agents' offices. The illustration is colorful and simple. It emphasizes visual ideas of calm and peace. The major slogan (the text) reinforces the visual message. It tells us how to get a similar peace of mind. Design by Adler, Schwartz Graphics, Inc.

BUILD A
$ 6897.30
NEST EGG
WITH LIFE
INSURANCE*

*Based on a $10,000 Life-Paid-to-65 policy.

YOUR INDEPENDENT **USF&G** AGENT
Representing Fidelity & Guaranty Life Insurance Co. / Thomas Jefferson Life Insurance Co.

Notice the simple combination of bold lettering and line drawing. Together they make this poster very successful. Lettering and the overlapping image are laid out to create a sense of unity and movement. Design by Adler, Schwartz Graphics, Inc.

In the posters you create, try different arrangements of lettering, illustrations and color. In one poster you might emphasize lettering. In another, you might attract attention through splashes of color or an attractive illustration. Whatever you do, remember that your design must reach out and stop the passerby! Otherwise, your efforts will not succeed.

Designing a Poster

A poster is designed to present one idea, one unified message. This may be done by combining a catchy slogan with a colorful illustration. Some posters, such as those advertising an event, include a date, time and admission price. As you design, follow a plan such as this:

1. Gather all the facts that must be in your poster: title, place, time, date, etc. Collect illustration ideas and everything that should be in the message.
2. Organize this information in terms of a slogan, an illustration and other necessary facts.
3. Determine the poster's size and shape. Decide which art medium might be used most successfully. Decide what paper or board would be best.
4. Start designing by making a series of many small, rough, pencil sketches of your poster ("thumbnails") about 2"×3" (5×8 cm).
5. Select several of these. Make preliminary sketches in proportion to the planned finished size. For the average poster, preliminary sketches may be approximately one-quarter scale. For example, if the finished poster is to be 20"×28" (51×71 cm), a good first sketch size is 5"×7" (12×18 cm).

The rough and preliminary sketches are the most important steps in designing your poster. This is where you try arrangements of lettering and illustration, styles and sizes of lettering, and color combinations. Develop these sketches carefully, so that the later ones look like miniature posters.

Balance

Review the elements and principles of design. What kind of balance would you like your design to follow? Symmetrical (formal) balance may be obtained by arranging the lettering and illustrations so that the left side is very similar to the right side.

Try planning the same poster using an asymmetrical or informal design. Symmetrical balance is thought more conservative and restful than asymmetrical. Both approaches can be used effectively. Usually more excitement can be generated with informal balance.

Along with balance, there are other design qualities that you should consider. The next pages will help you organize the elements of your posters so that your designs are effective.

A sample poster announces a flower show. The show is put on by students in the gardening class. First gather the text.

1. Title: Student Flower Show
   Place: Gymnasium
   Date: May 15
   Time: 3:30 PM
   Illustration idea: flowers of some kind

2. A slogan for the poster could be "Student Flower Show." It could also be something like, "Treat Your Senses." Flowers will be the image, either painted in tempera or cut from colored paper. Include some information about the gardening class in small type.

3. The size will be 28" × 22" (51 × 71 cm), on posterboard. The board's color will depend on the design.

4. Start work by making rough, thumbnail sketches. Those shown here are actual size. Make a dozen or more.

A

B

C

Choose your favorite thumbnail sketches. Make preliminary sketches for the poster. The three illustrations
above show how line drawing can be used to begin.
Each illustration shows balance: A is symmetrical. B and
C are asymmetrical.

The illustrations differ in their emphasis. A balances illustration and words, especially with similar colors and values. B emphasizes the illustration, especially if it is
brightly-colored. C emphasizes the words. Each can be
effective. Choose only one for further development.

Emphasis

Emphasize only one thing in your poster. Arrange the
other poster parts so that they catch the eye in de-
scending order of importance. For example, if the illustration is most important, make it large and bold.
Then make the lettering smaller, so it becomes less
important.

You may wish to emphasize the lettering. In this
case, design the illustration so it is less important in
size or color.

You can use emphasis within the lettering. Perhaps
one word is the most important part of a slogan. Focus attention on *this* word by making it larger, a different type style or a different color. Experiment by
creating small color sketches before you begin to
make the real poster.

Try using background panels or shapes to emphasize words or illustrations. Generous use of open
space also will focus attention on parts you wish to
emphasize.

The asymmetrical balance in this design adds action and excitement. The car seems to be driving off the billboard. How does the design emphasize the word "RENAULT" and the price? Notice the simple use of words and slogan. The corporation logo is in the lower right corner.

This design is symmetrically balanced. Dynamic emphasis comes from the car perched atop the building. It is hard to miss such a visual impact. The words overlap the illustration. This provides unity, as does the gray shape with faces. Imagine how disordered the design would be with nine heads floating in white space. The corporation logo is in the lower right corner.

Unity

Although you may emphasize one component in your poster, all of the parts (text, symbols, colors, illustrations) should be designed so that they form a single unit. Plan for this so that your poster will not look disorganized. Even if the lettering is perfect, the slogan well-worded and the illustration very effective, if the elements are not unified, the poster will fail.

You might achieve unity by overlapping the slogan and the illustration. Try using background panels or colored shapes that join the illustration and lettering to produce unity. Treat the background as a single area or shape of color. This can aid unity. So will use of a similar style, technique or color in type and illustration. For example, if the color used in lettering and illustration is outlined with black, unity is established.

Movement

Arrange the parts of your poster so that people can't help moving their eyes from one part of it to another in a sequence you plan. For example, think about grouping the individual elements (illustration, slogan, other lettering) so that there is natural movement from the illustration, to slogan, to most important words, to the *most important word*.

You can create movement with directional arrows, lines and lines of dots. Use an action illustration that points the observer's eyes in a desired direction. Create movement with gradations of color, large letters that direct the eye, or the poster's overall shape.

Try several arrangements. Put the center of interest in several positions in your thumbnail sketches. Then

These three preliminary sketches stress unity. A *is a symmetrical design. The overlapping letters are tied to the illustration. In* B *purple background shapes unite words and illustration. A lighter value of purple would be more effective. In* C, *style unites the illustration and major lettering. They are in the same technique—shapes of color and type outlined in black. The even text margins provide more unity.*

A

B

How have unity and movement been created here? This is a television graphic for a Denver station. How did the artist pull the major bunch of flowers forward from the background? This makes them more important. Notice the simple type style. Why is this important on a television title?

add the rest of the required parts. Each thumbnail sketch will have a different path of movement. Which do you like best?

In the examples on this page, notice how the blocks of words often are lined up. Their edges are even. This provides movement and adds a feeling of organization. Without this, words would seem to tumble and the poster would lack unity.

The black arrows show how design movement leads your eye through this preliminary sketch. Your view moves from curved flower stems to flowers (which point downward), to the slogan and the word "senses." This word stands out because it is larger than the others.

C

This four-sided bus route poster is a permanent street fixture. It provides information for the public. Lettering is simple and readable. The diagram is efficient and accurate. The large 86 is the route number. It is the most important feature. Local Service Westbound to Van Nuys explains where bus 86 goes. Design by Saul Bass and Associates.

This newspaper advertisement is an excellent example of graphic design. The design would make an effective poster, too. Visual movement begins with the bold figure, goes up the raised arm and then down the ski pole to the lettering. The type style of the store (Robinson's) and the manufacturer (Fila) are well-known trademarks. The product is emphasized more than the store. How is this done? The details are in small type, available to those who are interested. The use of illustration, type, layout and open space make this very effective. Design by Stephen Bieck.

The Arco lettering is part of the company logo. Look carefully at the type for am pm mini market. It draws attention to itself when surrounded by bolder and blockier typestyles. Color illustrates the idea of day and night (am and pm). This reinforces the written idea.

Specific Appeal

Show clearly the meaning (purpose) of your poster. Do this through choices of lettering, style, illustration and colors. A poster promoting a carnival would have bright colors and lively symbols. A Halloween Dance poster will be quite different from a poster for a graduation dinner.

Study the work of professional graphic designers. An advertisement for an expensive automobile will have a quiet, classic feeling of luxury. An advertisement for a four-wheel drive truck might stress strength, durability and adventurous excitement. The car might even be called a "motor car," the truck a "fun vehicle." The lettering for the car ad may be flowing and elegant. That for the truck may be blocky, bold and heavy. Designers plan these details carefully. They all help communicate the meaning of their graphic design. Think about this as you plan your poster.

Aqua Vend is a company that sells drinking water. Dispensers are placed in front of supermarkets. The lettering on this poster is right for the product. The lettering style combines type and illustration (wave symbols for water) in one unit. Notice how the upper and lowercase letters combine in an effective type design. The color is as cool and refreshing as the water.

Open Space and Simplicity

A poster should be uncluttered, with lots of open space. This is much easier to read than a poster whose words are hard to find.

Study advertisements, billboards and professional posters. The most effective ones have key words that can be read from a distance. Less important words and details are clear only at close range. You can see the key words best if they are placed in open space. If key words are crowded by other words or don't have enough contrast, the poster is unsuccessful. Open space allows words to stand out. This prevents confusion.

Lettering

In general, lettering should be simple, attractive and easy to read. Beyond that, you have a lot of choices. Letters may be bold or light, straight or slanted, condensed (squeezed together) or extended (spread out). You may use all capital letters, two sizes of capitals, all small letters or a combination.

Letters must be uniform in size and on a straight line. Light pencil guidelines will help you get these results.

Generally avoid tricky lettering, vertical arrangements and words placed at sharp angles. Horizontal lettering is the most *readable*. Readability is the most important quality.

There are expressive words such as *fast*, *slow*, *cold* and *hot*. You can shape the letters to reflect each word's meaning. How can you draw the word *fast* so that it really looks like it is moving fast? Try it.

Remember, the lettering on your poster is as important as the illustration. Poor lettering can ruin an otherwise excellent poster.

You can create letters using pen and ink, markers or paint and brush. You can cut them from colored paper. Art supply stores carry sheets of letters that you can press onto posters. You can use these to create words that look machine-printed.

You can make letters freehand, or you can draw them carefully before coloring or inking. This depends on the needs of the poster, your design and your lettering skill. Even graffiti-style lettering can be used well in some designs.

Study type styles and words in magazine advertisements. Cut out styles that you find attractive. Choose from among them as you design your posters. When you begin to letter your posters, use your collection as models.

American Typewriter Bold

American Typewriter Medium Condensed

Cathedral

Block Condensed

Company

Delphin No I

El Greco

Flamenco Inline

Frankfurter Medium

Gillies Gothic Bold

Le Golf

Mendoza Demi Gras

POSTER design

Color

Select colors that will support the poster's idea. You do not have to use every color in a single design. Some posters that have only one or two colors are more effective that those with many colors. Remember that you can have a variety of values from only one color.

Think about the meaning and effect of each color. Blues and greens are refreshing and cool. Yellows, reds and oranges are warm and active. Cool colors recede. Warm colors advance.

Look carefully. The large bottle is actually painted on a flat surface. The painted shadows provide a startling realism. The lettering is simple, appropriate, classical and effective. The colors are cool and refreshing, as is the product.

Many colors have symbolic meaning. Red is often used to show danger, power or a signal to stop. Green means go. Purple refers to royalty. Blue refers to truth and yellow to caution. You can apply these properties to your design.

Colors also affect each other. Yellow on white will appear different from yellow on black. Related colors, such as red and orange, produce more subtle relationships than complementary colors, such as orange and blue. Complementary colors provide great visual contrast. Through your color choice, you can create varying levels of contrast. You must select colors carefully to establish mood and unity.

Experiment with color. Try different combinations such as light on dark, bright with dull or large areas of one color with smaller amounts of a contrasting color.

Signs of the zodiac and travel posters can contain only one word. Visit a travel office to pick up old travel posters. This poster has white and black painted lines over a tissue paper collage.

Completing Your Poster

Make many thumbnail sketches. Explore several directions for your poster. Make several preliminary color sketches, and decide which will be most useful. Ask yourself several questions.

Which sketch best presents the idea?
Does it tell the message?
Is the design brief, direct and complete?
Will it attract attention?
Is it easy to read?

If your answers are satisfactory, begin your full-sized poster.

Make a full-sized sketch on a large sheet of paper. The sheet should be the size of the finished poster. If your preliminary sketch is one-quarter scale, enlarge everything four times as you make the full-size sketch. Make all your adjustments and corrections. Then trace the full-size drawing onto a sheet of posterboard.

You may want to avoid the intermediate step and lay out your design directly on the posterboard. In either case, use a soft pencil to create guidelines for the most important lettering. Be sure the size is in proportion to the final sketch. Then position the illustrations and draw in the letters.

Only after this, or after you have traced the full-size drawing onto the posterboard, complete your poster. Will you use tempera paints, colored paper, felt markers, pen and ink or watercolor? Follow your color sketch as you choose final colors. When the coloring is complete, use an art gum eraser (or any soft eraser) to erase the guidelines and remove other lines or smudges.

This movie billboard is a huge poster. It uses a realistic illustration to attract attention. The verbal message is simple and effective. The design is symmetrical, though the illustration is not. How is this possible? What devices provide unity?

Variations

Try combining colored paper and paint. You can paste a large background paper shape onto the poster board and paint your illustration on that. You can letter your slogan on a long piece of colored paper. Would you use light paint on dark paper? You can cut the slogan's letters from colored paper and paste them in position.

Experiment with different materials and techniques. You may even try building up the surface of the poster board to create three-dimensional effects.

Have fun trying many variations and combinations. Remember though the basic principle of postermaking: Keep the message simple and easy to read.

Two student posters feature cut-out letters. The designs provide unity and simplicity while making bold statements.

14 Crafts

Bright colors and yarns of several thicknesses make this seventh grader's off-loom weaving especially striking.

There is drama, even magic, in the world of crafts. Perhaps it comes from the challenge of creating with so many fascinating materials and processes. It may be the thrill of making something with your own hands. Whatever the product, the process of designing and working with crafts materials can be an exciting experience.

Begin by reading this section and studying the pictures. Get to know the tools, materials and techniques of different crafts. Begin to discover the many kinds of crafts objects: jewelry, wall hangings, bowls, vases, trays, even mosaic table tops.

After reviewing the many possibilities in crafts, decide what item you would like to make. Then concentrate on its design and construction. Select the materials that contribute visually and structurally. Often there will be a range from which to select. For example, jewelry may be made from wood, metal, paper, cloth, clay or combinations.

Design Suggestions

After selecting your crafts area, make decisions for each of these:

1. Specific object that you will design and create (ring, pendant, scarf, hand bag, ceramic bowl, wall hanging, etc.
2. Materials and tools that you will need.
3. Techniques or processes to be used. A wall hanging, for example, might be made by weaving, stitching, batik or combinations of these.
4. Development of your design.

   Review the elements and principles of design. Study the range of designs in the work of professional craftspeople. Look again at the illustrations on

This lidded pot was created by Harrison McIntosh. It can hold candy or other things. It is also beautiful enough to be admired for its form and subtle glazes. Courtesy Louis Newman Galleries, Beverly Hills.

An Indian potter, Maria Martinez, made this and other black-on-black bowls and plates. They are useful and they are highly prized by art collectors. The Indian Art Center of California.

Trimming greenware is part of the ceramic process. This student is carving a foot on her coil-made bowl.

these pages. Review reference books, prints and actual crafts objects. Study natural forms (flowers, trees, leaves, rocks) to see how their intricate structures may be adapted to your design. Discover the traits and possibilities of your materials.

Make several preliminary sketches. Choose the size, shape and character of your design. Include color combinations, surface treatment and other details as you think it over.

Keep your design simple. Remember its ultimate use and its decorative value. Consider the shapes and layout that will achieve unity. Plan to use line to give a feeling of movement. Plan textures to provide smoothness, roughness and variety. Create a design you really like.

It will help if you practice certain skills (sawing metal, joining and texturing clay, basic stitches). The more skillful you become with your tools and materials, the more you will enjoy using them and creating artwork.

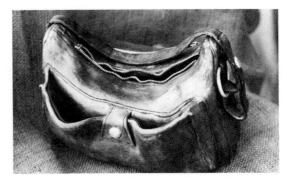

A student used slabs of clay to create this realistic handbag, complete with zipper and snap.

Jewelry

Gold, silver and precious stones are traditionally associated with jewelry. This section will explore fairly low-cost materials. The value of an item can depend very little on expensive materials. Your design and skill are most important.

First consider originality of design, color and attractiveness. Study the designs in these pages. Look at jewelry in stores, craft shops, museums and galleries. Do several "thumbnail" sketches of your own design. Gather your basic materials, and collect various useful odds and ends (nuts, bolts, small gears, washers, buttons, beads, discarded costume jewelry).

Joseph Gatto crafted this unique gold ring. His design exhibits the ancient scarab. The scarab was created by an Egptian artisan who lived about 3000 years ago.

This is a finely-crafted Navajo rug. The weaving is of such high quality that it might be collected by a museum. The Indian Art Center of California.

Textured and painted papier-mâché discs form this necklace.

Paper Jewelry

Basic materials: newspaper, paper napkins, paper towels, colored tissue; wheat paste, white glue; cardboard sheets and tubing; yarn, string, cord; old or broken pieces of costume jewelry; tempera paints, shellac, acrylic paints; small brushes.

Paper jewelry techniques make use of paper pulp, laminated paper and cardboard forms.

For the **paper pulp** method, soak small bits of newspaper in a bucket of water overnight. Drain off the water, squeezing out the excess. Add wheat paste as a binder. The resulting pastelike material (paper pulp) can be used to make beads of varying sizes.

Roll the pulp into balls. While the beads are wet, punch a hole through each with a piece of wire or a toothpick. Try making some beads that are cube-shaped, oval or cylindrical.

When dry, the beads may be painted or covered with colored tissue and thinned white glue. Use your imagination. Try decorating larger beads by painting them with lines, shapes, colors, words, or faces. If you use tempera paints, coat the beads with shellac after the paint is dry. **Do not breathe shellac fumes. Do not get shellac on your skin. Follow safety precautions on the container.** Acrylic paints are permanent and do not need shellac.

Experiment with paper pulp to make small sculpted forms for pendants and earrings. What other ways can you think of to create paper pulp jewelry?

Ceramic Jewelry

Basic materials: clay, Egyptian paste; objects for creating textures, such as forks, gears, wire mesh, saw blades, nails; rolling pin; wood strips (1/4″ × 18″; .6cm × 46cm); glazes, kiln.

Clay lends itself to many techniques for making jewelry.

You can shape clay into balls, cubes or long forms to make beads or earrings. Experiment with clay coils or narrow strips. How can you use these in your design? Remember to make a hole in beads.

Place a large lump of clay on a flat surface. Put two long wood strips parallel on each side of the clay. Using a rolling pin, roll out a slab of clay. Cut your designed shapes from the slab. Create textures on each to complete the surface decoration.

Roll another slab of clay. Build up the surface with more clay or carve into the surface.

Ceramic jewelry may be finished by bisque firing and then staining or glaze firing. When glaze firing, beads should be strung on nichrome wire. Position them in the kiln so that none of them touch.

Egyptian paste is a special clay. It is widely used in jewelry making, particularly for beads. It is a combination of clay and glaze. It is bought as a powder and mixed with water. You can use it to make beads of many sizes and shapes.

Pendants of this kind have aluminum foil over cardboard shapes. India ink was brushed on and wiped off to provide the interesting patina.

These ceramic pendants are shown after bisque firing. They were decorated by pressing carved plaster "stamps" into the soft clay forms. Can you think of other things to press into clay for interesting textures?

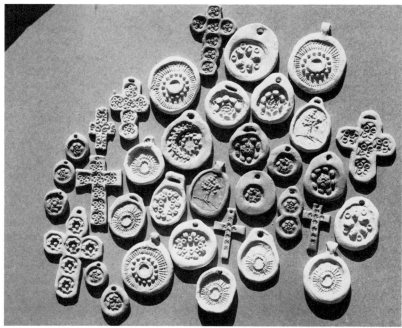

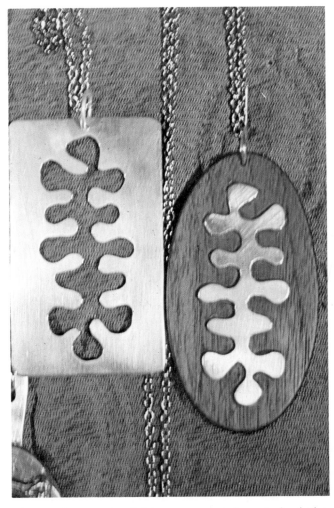

The pendant on the right uses a wood shape to back the metal design. The design was cut from the silver sheet on the left. Notice the use of positive and negative shapes in these two works.

Wood Jewelry

Basic materials: hard woods such as walnut and rosewood; soft woods such as white pine; coping saws, wood files, hand drill, bits; sandpaper; stains, paints, brushes.

Although it is rigid, wood can be used for making many kinds of jewelry, including cuff links, pendants and unusual necklaces. Wood may also be used with other materials. A pendant may have a copper-enameled shape mounted on a contrasting wood shape. You could make a necklace with alternating ceramic and wood beads.

Wood may be sawed, carved, filed and pieced together with glue. You can finish it by sanding and applying a clear finish. You can paint it with acrylic or enamel paints, or you can stain it. **Spray or stain only in an area with active ventilation.** You may paint a design on the surface of larger pieces.

These ebony wood shapes on a copper chain were created by Edith Crawford. The shapes are separated by small pieces of copper tubing.

Clay

Clay is one of the oldest materials used to make practical and decorative forms. It is one of the most satisfying and popular materials. Clay has wonderful *plasticity* —a ready response to varying pressures.

Experiment with a ball of clay. Select a chunk about the size of a large orange. How does the clay feel in your hands? Squeeze it. What happens? Punch your thumb or a finger into the clay ball. Pinch and pull some of the clay out from the ball without breaking it off. Cut the ball apart and smash it together again.

Place the clay ball on a sheet of masonite or board, covered with a closely woven cloth or the reverse side of a piece of oil cloth. Press down on your clay. Flatten it. Pull a small piece of clay from the ball. Roll it out with the flat part of your hand. Starting at one end of this long, snake-like strip of clay, coil it so that it is similar to a coil of rope or the mainspring of a watch.

Roll the clay back into a ball. Cut it into slices about ¼" thick. Can you join these flat circles or discs of clay to create an interesting arrangement?

Start again with a ball of clay. Using the entire chunk, move it around in your hands, changing its shape. Pull some clay out. Push other areas in. Think of a humorous figure or fantasy animal. Continue this until you feel satisfied that your clay figure is finished. Try not to break off or add any clay.

How do you feel about clay now? Can you describe some of its properties? Would you agree that your hands are the most important tools you have for shaping and reshaping clay? Did you enjoy experimenting with the ball of clay?

Experiments, such as the ones suggested here, will help you understand the properties of clay. As you design and make clay objects, use these discoveries in your work.

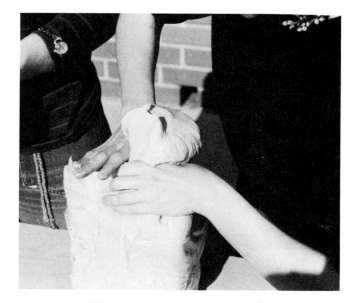

The handsome ceramic pot seen here is in its greenware stage. It was made of coils and then carved, formed and textured to create this amusing product.

The artist used many kinds of tools to imprint, carve and press textures into the surface of this imaginary fish.

Materials and Tools

Materials include wet ceramic clay, lead-free under-glazes and glazes (for decorating), slip (clay in liquid form) and plastic bags (for work in progress).

You will need a work surface of modeling board (pressed wood) or oilcloth to cover the table; cutting and forming tools (paring knife, tongue depressors, wood and wire clay tools); sponges; cans for water; objects for texturing clay (nails, sticks, spools, dowels, jar tops, wire mesh, gears, corrugated board, saw blades or comb).

Probably you will have "ready-to-use" clay. This comes packaged in a twenty-five or fifty-pound plastic container. You should prepare this clay by removing air pockets (which can explode your piece during firing). This insures proper consistency. Remove air pockets in one of two ways.

1. ***Kneading*** Work with a large, flat chunk of clay. Pull part of it back with the fingers of both hands. Then fold the piece over the other part and press it all back together with your palms. This is much like a baker kneading dough. Repeat this until you feel that the clay can be used for modeling.

2. ***Wedging*** Form a large ball of clay. Pat it with your palms. Cut the clay ball in half with a piece of thin wire. Many wedging boards have a wire attached for this purpose. Notice how many air pockets you reveal. Put one piece on the wedging board. Slam the other half on top of it. This action will break air bubbles in the clay. Repeat the process until the clay, when cut, appears to have an even texture with no air pockets.

Surface Decorating Techniques

The surface of a clay object is as important as the form. Whatever technique you choose, design the surface so that it relates to the total design.

The surface of a clay pot, for example, may be smooth (use a sponge, fingers and water). Or it may be textured. You can press objects into it or scratch across it. The texture will depend on how you use your objects.

There are other surface decoration and finishing techniques for clay. These include the use of underglaze colors, glaze colors, and underglazes combined with clear glaze. Underglaze colors are muted (dull or earthen). They are made of liquid clay. When fired they have a dull finish. If you want a high shine, coat the object with a clear glaze over the underglaze colors and refire it. You can paint a shape on the surface of a clay piece using a contrasting underglaze color. When this dries, use a pointed object to scratch a design through the added color into the basic clay. This technique is known as *sgraffito*.

Glazes are available in a variety of colors and a wide range of brilliance. When fired, different types of glazes become glossy, mottled or crackled. Glazes may be applied with a brush or by spraying, dripping, pouring and dunking. **Be sure to use only lead-free glazes.**

Paul Bellardo formed this vase on a potter's wheel. Then he worked the greenware surface to create a striking overall textured pattern.

This student is using a brush and water to join a coil border to her coil-built pot.

Several pinch pots were joined together. They create a single, sculptural unit.

This ceramic vase was built over a bottle. The artist pressed chunks of clay together around the bottle. The bottle was removed and a bottom was added. The artist carved a linoleum block and pressed the design on a clay slab. Then the slab was attached to the vase.

Firing

When your piece is modelled, let it dry at room temperature. This may take several days, depending on the room's humidity and the thickness of the clay. At this point the clay piece is called *greenware*. The first firing of greenware (without glaze) is called *bisque firing*. The piece is then called *bisqueware*. During the bisque firing the clay matures (hardens). Glazes may then be added to the surface of the bisqueware and the pieces fired again.

Completely dried greenware is placed in a kiln for bisque firing (above). The fired bisqueware is removed from the cooled kiln (below). It is ready for staining, glazing or other finishing.

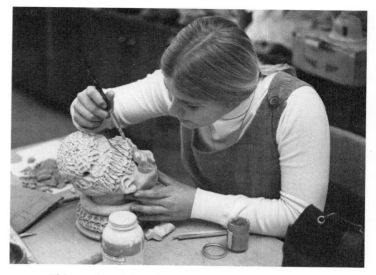

This student is brushing glazes onto her bisqueware ceramic sculpture. It will be fired again to produce the finished product.

Two Hand-building Techniques

Pinch pot   Hold a ball of clay. At one point press your thumbs into it. Turn the ball as you continue to press your thumbs in. Gradually pull outward until you have a bowl or cup shape. How can you finish this pinch pot? Try making two or three pinch pots and joining them into a single unit. How many different ways can you join two pinch pots?

Coil   The coil technique constructs a desired form (bowl, figure) with coils of clay. As you build coil to coil, crosshatch both surfaces, add slip and press together. In the finished piece, you may leave the coil forms as a major feature, or you may wish to smooth the surface. Coils are usually made by rolling clay on a flat surface with the palm of your hand. For a different effect, make a slab of clay one fourth of an inch thick. Cut narrow strips ¼″ to ½″ wide from the slab. How could these be used as coils in constructing a pot?

Coil combined with pinch pot   Now that you have used these two techniques separately, you can try combining them. Try making a pot (vase) 8″ (20 cm) high. Use the pinch pot technique to construct the base. Complete the pot by adding coils.

This coiled ceramic vase was not glazed. It was stained with an umber colorant.

238

You can combine colorful yarns with other materials. Here twigs were used to produce interesting wall hangings.

Putting Personal Ideas into Clay

Use your experience with pinch pot, coil and a combination of the two techniques to design and make a variety of items. Stretch your imagination. Aim for the unusual.

Fiber Arts

Fiber art is an ancient craft that at one time was done entirely by hand. Textiles today are produced on a large scale by massive automated machinery. Public demand for fabrics along with amazing advances in industrial technology caused this automation. Think of the many uses for textiles. In addition to clothes, how many things in your house are made of fabric? Walk through a local department store and make a list of those products which are made partly or entirely of cloth. You may be surprised by the length of your list.

Despite the technology, individually designed and created textiles is a thriving craft at this point in history. The pride and joy of designing and making your own things cannot be replaced by a machine.

The discussion of textiles in this section of the book is divided into two design categories: one in which the design is an integral part of the fabric (weaving) and one in which the design is applied to the surface of an existing piece of cloth (stichery), tie-dye, tie-bleach). There are other design techniques but try these first.

Weaving

Weaving may have originated with cavepeople trying to protect themselves from damp cave floors. They discovered that by interlocking grasses they could make crude floor mats.

Weaving is based on the interlacing of threads, referred to as the *warp*, with other threads (yarn, cloth strips) that are called *weft*. There are several approaches to weaving from non-loom techniques to simple looms to the more complex harness looms. But you should first explore ideas with one technique. Then try to improve your design and weaving skills by using other techniques. Review design suggestions in the beginning of this chapter and the elements and principles of design presented earlier.

Weaving materials Yarns (wool, cotton, synthetic) for the *weft* are available in many colors. Warp yarns

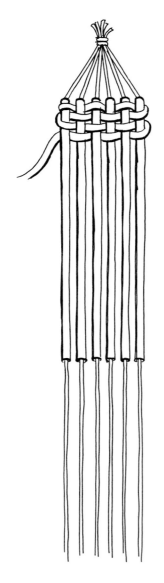

Straw loom.

Cardboard loom.

of strong cord may be used for warping the loom. Scissors and materials to construct a specific type of loom are also needed.

Straw loom The straw loom is a very simple technique for weaving belts or bands.

Start by cutting six lengths of heavy cord or yarn longer than the belt or band you want. Thread each of these cords through six straws. The straws should be cut in half. An easy way to get the cord through the straw is to insert it at one end and then suck the straw from the other end. After doing this, tie the six cords together at one end, allowing the other ends to hang free.

With the six straws pushed tightly against the knotted end, weave with your favorite color of yarn, over and under the straws, back and forth. Keep the weft threads close together. As you continue to weave, you may wish to change the color of your weft. Select another color of yarn. Tie the yarn to the first color and weave it into your design.

When the straws become partly filled, push the woven part up off the top of the straws to provide more space for your weaving. When your design is complete, slip the straws off the remaining bits of warp. Tie the loose ends together, add a buckle and try on your new belt.

This is a simple technique but it allows you to explore the basic principle of weaving. As you explore other weaving methods, think of ways to add variety and interest to your work. Be innovative. What other materials could you use to make your design unusual?

Students wove these small tapestries. The students used colorful yarns and several weaving techniques.

A wood frame loom is illustrated above. Looms such as this are used for weavings such as the student work shown below.

Cardboard looms can be made in any shape and size. This colorful work is on a round cardboard loom.

Notice many kinds of stitches and several kinds of thread here. A student artist created this city scene with a radiant sun.

Cardboard loom Cardboard looms are made from any kind of rigid, heavy cardboard (bookbinder's board, corrugated box board). The major difference in cardboard looms is the size. The size of the loom determines the size of your weaving.

Cut a rectangular shape of cardboard, 8"×10" (20 cm×25 cm). Cut an uneven number of notches, ¼" apart, across two opposite ends. Tape one end of the warp thread to the back of the cardboard. Starting with the first notch at one end, string the warp thread across the cardboard to the opposite notch. Go around the first notch to the second notch and across the cardboard to the opposite second notch. Continue this until the entire loom is covered with a series of parallel warp threads. Then tie the two ends of the warp thread together. Your loom is now ready

Box loom (similar to wooden frame).

242

for weaving. Select your weaving (weft) materials and proceed. Think of ways to add interest to your design as you move the weft yarns over and under the warp. What materials could you use other than yarn?

Prepare a cardboard loom by wrapping the warp thread around both sides. Then weave on both sides. Try other shapes of cardboard. Could you do the same thing with a round piece of cardboard? Try it.

Wood frame loom   Construct a wood frame loom with strips of wood (a picture frame will serve the purpose). Drive a straight row of brads (small nails), about ¼″ apart, across opposite ends of the loom. Tie the warp thread around the first nail at either end. Then string the warp back and forth, tying it at the final nail. Start weaving.

There are many other types of looms. Those described here offer a wide range of possibilities.

Stitchery

Stitchery is different from weaving. Stitchery is the technique of designing *on* cloth. Think of it as drawing or painting with stitches.

You can design stitchery for wall hangings, banners and other decorative items. Useful objects such as soft containers (shoulder bags, hand bags, shopping bags) can be made with stitchery techniques. Would you like to plan a design for a blouse or a shirt? What other items are suitable for stitchery designs?

Practice the basic stitches (running, chain, couching, satin, blanket, cross, feather) on a piece of cloth. As you master these, start inventing your own. Think of ways that you can use stitches in your own design ideas. Then plan a design and complete it with a variety of stitches. Refer to design suggestions presented earlier in this section of the book. Again, it would be helpful to review the elements and principles of design.

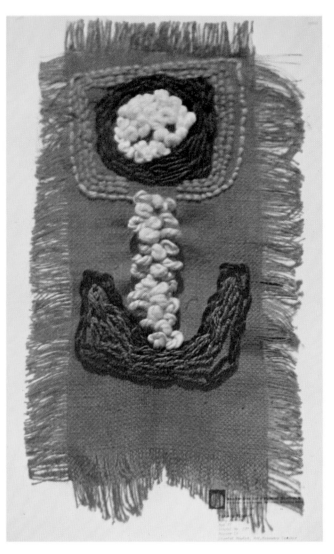

Select yarns and fabrics that go well together. Be imaginative in your stitching techniques.

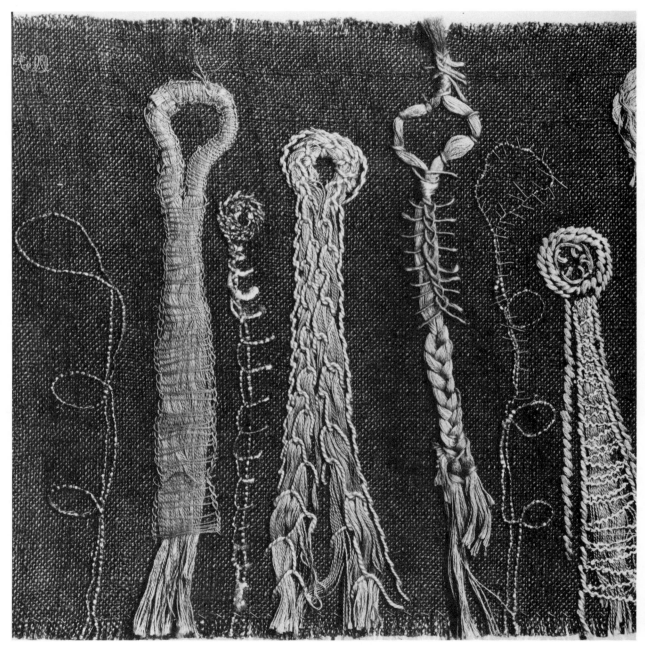

A variety of exciting stitches and techniques make up this stitchery design. A student created it with combinations of basic stitches and imaginative variations.

Basic Stitches for Creative Stitchery

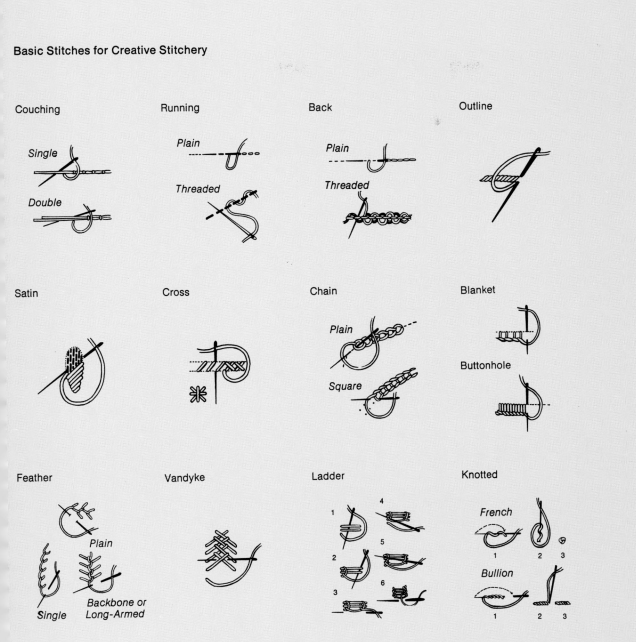

Couching
- *Single*
- *Double*

Running
- *Plain*
- *Threaded*

Back
- *Plain*
- *Threaded*

Outline

Satin

Cross

Chain
- *Plain*
- *Square*

Blanket

Buttonhole

Feather
- *Plain*
- *Single*
- *Backbone or Long-Armed*

Vandyke

Ladder

Knotted
- *French*
- *Bullion*

Above, the cloth is tied and prepared for dyeing. Below, a finished tie-dye design shows typical tie-dye patterns.

You will be stitching with yarns and threads but you can get interesting results by including other things into your design. Try beads, buttons or old pieces of costume jewelry.

Materials and tools   Fabric for the background (monks cloth, burlap, cotton cloth, denim); yarn, thread, embroidery floss, jute, cord; beads, buttons, discarded pieces of costume jewelry, washers, found objects; suitable needles.

Tie-Dye

Tie-dye is similar to the ancient craft of batik. Tie-dye combines blocking out parts of the cloth with dyeing to produce a design. The name itself describes the process. Design results are obtained by the way cloth is folded and tied. The accidental way the dye runs often contributes to the finished design. Instead of wax (a resist material used in batik design), the blocking out is done by the way in which the cloth is folded and tied.

Experiment with a piece of cloth. Bunch up one section of it. Tie it tightly, wrapping the cord around it several times. You may repeat this in several different parts of the cloth. Dip the tied cloth in a con-

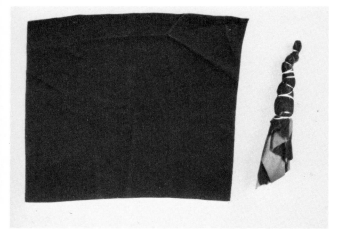

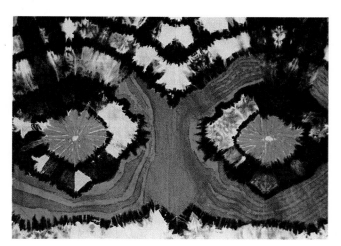

At left are a dark piece of material and a tied cloth, ready for bleaching. On the right notice the typical patterns of the tie-bleach technique.

tainer of dye and then hang it up to dry. **Handle dyes carefully. Some are toxic.** After it has dried, remove the cord and enjoy your design.

This is the basic process of tie-dye. Can you get different kinds of design by the way in which you fold and tie the cloth? Can you use more than one color of dye? Try to dye just the folded part of the cloth. Use different folding techniques.

Materials   Any plain cotton cloth is suitable. After you have had success on pieces of cloth, you may wish to tie-dye a plain blouse, shirt or other article of clothing. You'll also need household dyes, large cans or buckets to hold the dyes and cord.

Tie-Bleach

The tie-bleach technique is similar to tie-dye except that tie-bleach requires cloth in a solid color. In tie-bleach, the cloth is tied and dipped in bleach to remove some of the original color and produce a design. You must be sure that the color in the cloth is not fast (resists the bleach).

How can tie-bleach be used on items that you would wear or carry? Could this technique be used for the designing and making of wall hangings? What else?

Combined Techniques

One of the most exciting things about design is exploring ideas beyond the basic processes. Try combining stitchery with tie-dye or tie-bleach. Would buttons, beads and parts of old, unused costume jewelry contribute to your design? What other combinations of materials and techniques can you think of?

Summary

Many techniques, processes and materials have been discussed in this section of the book. They are only a part of the larger world of crafts. There are more complex crafts that you may wish to study. The basic skills you have learned can be used with more advanced techniques.

The important thing is that you look at crafts objects in museums, stores and book illustrations. This will expand your understanding of the many ways that craftspeople create designs and use materials. Be aware of crafts as an important part of contemporary life as well as past cultures. Think of crafts not only as practical objects but as designs that add beauty to your life. Try many different crafts materials and continue to use crafts techniques for your own art ideas.

Glossary

abstract art   a style of art that uses simplified arrangements of shape, line, texture and color, often geometric to depict people, places or objects. *Abstract* may refer to nonobjective art.

Abstract Expressionism   a twentieth-century painting style that expresses feelings and emotions through slashing, active brushstrokes. Often called *Action Painting*.

acropolis   the highest point of any ancient Greek city and the site of the temples. The *Parthenon* is on the acropolis in Athens.

aesthetic   dealing with the nature of beauty and artistic judgments.

aqueduct   a long, continuous trough built by the ancient Romans to bring water from the mountains to cities by gravity. The aqueducts crossed valleys on tall bridges that included arches.

architect   a person who designs and creates plans for buildings, groups of buildings or communities.

architecture   the design of buildings, such as homes, offices, schools, industrial structures.

artifacts   objects usually simple, that were created or adapted by people.

assemblage   artwork that includes various three-dimensional objects. It can stand on the floor or hang on a wall.

asymmetrical balance   a type of visual balance in which the two sides of the composition are different yet balanced; visually equal without being identical.

Avant Garde Art   the style of *contemporary* art at any time. It is the newest form of visual expression, and farthest from traditional ways of working.

balance   a principle of design that refers to the equalization of elements. There are three kinds of balance: symmetrical (formal), asymmetrical (informal) and radial.

Baroque   a period of time (1600s) and style of art that stressed swirling action, large works of art and elaborate detail and richness, even in drawing.

basilica   an ancient Roman building (long and narrow) that served as a meeting place and judgement hall. Later, the Christians used the basilica style for their churches.

Bauhaus   A German art school, begun in 1918, that stressed science and technology as major resources for art and architecture.

bisque ware   a clay object that has been fired to appropriate temperature in a kiln.

brayer   a small roller used to spread printing ink on a linoleum block or wood block before printing.

Byzantine Art   the art style of Byzantium, using a lot of gold and mosaic in church decorations.

Byzantium   an ancient Greek and Roman city on the Bosporus, now called Istanbul, Turkey. Constantine used it as the capital of the Eastern Roman Empire from 330 A.D., and changed its name to Constantinople.

cathedral   a large church for the congregation of a Roman Catholic Bishop. It contains his throne, called a *cathedra*.

ceramic jewelry   jewelry made from wet clay.

chroma   an element of design that relates to the brightness and dullness of a color.

cityscape   a painting or drawing that uses elements of the city (buildings, streets, shops) as subject matter.

collage   a technique in which the artist glues material (paper, cloth, found objects) to a background.

color   an element of design that identifies hues.

combine painting a type of painting begun in the twentieth century. The artist combines real objects (shirt, book, stuffed animal) with painted areas.

communication letting others know what you are thinking, saying and feeling. Communication may be verbal, visual, musical or physical.

composition the arrangement of the parts in a work of art, usually according to the principles of design.

conceptualized art a style of painting or sculpture. The artist communicates a general idea, not how the subject actually looks. An African tribal mask is a conceptualized face.

construction a product in which parts are added together to complete the work.

constructivism a style of art (1913) that stressed the three-dimensional, abstract arrangement of metals, glass, plastics and/or wire.

contemporary of the present time or style.

contrast a principle of design that refers to differences in values, colors, textures and other elements in an artwork. Contrast is used to achieve emphasis and interest.

contour drawing a single-line drawing that defines the outer and inner forms (contours) of the subject.

crafts a form of art expression through creation of useful objects. Can include fiber arts, ceramics and metal smithing.

craftsperson an artist who designs and creates useful objects such as textiles, ceramics and jewelry.

crayon etching a technique in which crayon is applied heavily to a ground, then covered with an opaque ink or paint. Designs are scratched (etched) through the covering material to the colored crayon below.

Cubism a style of art in which the subject is broken and reassembled in an abstract form, emphasizing geometric shapes.

culture those elements that add to the aesthetic aspects of our lives, enriching them with beauty and enjoyment.

dynasty a period of time in which a single family has dominance over a people, such as the Ming Dynasty in China.

emphasis a principle of design by which the artist or designer may use opposing sizes or shapes, contrasting colors or other means to draw greater attention to certain areas in a work of art.

etching a printmaking technique that transfers the inked image to paper from lines cut in a metal (or plastic) plate. The process needs a strong press.

expressionism any style of art in which the artist tries to communicate strong personal and emotional feelings. If written with a capital "E," it refers to a definite style of art begun in Germany early in the twentieth century.

fashion illustrator a person who draws fashion designs for advertisements in magazines and newspapers.

Fauvism a style of painting, started in France, in which the artist communicates feelings through a personal use of color, usually bright and intense.

firing the heating of ceramic clay in a kiln to harden the clay object.

fixative a substance that is sprayed over charcoal, pastel or pencil drawings to make those materials adhere permanently to the paper and to prevent smearing.

flying buttress a feature of Gothic architecture made up of a tower buttress, standing away from the wall of the church, and a flying arch, connecting the buttress to the wall.

form an element of three-dimensional design (cube, sphere, pyramid, cylinder and free flowing) enclosing volume. Contrasts with the design element *shape*, which is two-dimensional (flat).

fresco a painting technique in which artists apply wet colored plaster to a wet plaster wall. A type of mural painting.

forum the center of a Roman city used as marketplace, for assemblies and for other business.

geometric art art that uses lines and shapes that recall geometry: triangles, squares, rectangles, straight lines, arcs, circles.

Gothic Art the art of Europe (1150 to 1400) mainly associated with church construction. It centered in France and spread over the continent. It is characterized by pointed arches, flying buttresses, stained glass windows and overall unity of construction.

Gothic arch a pointed arch, developed to allow greater height in building and huge window spaces in Gothic churches.

gouges scoop-shaped tools used for removing linoleum or wood when making relief print blocks of these materials.

graphic artist a person who designs packages and advertisements for newspapers and magazines; illustrates for ads, books, magazines; draws cartoons; designs displays and signs; produces any kind of art for reproduction.

greenware a clay piece that has dried, usually at room temperature.

grog fired stoneware that is ground and added to fresh wet clay to give it more body and texture.

ground the surface on which two-dimensional artwork is done, such as paper, canvas, cardboard.

hard edge painting   a style of art in which the artist uses crisp, clean edges and applies the values or colors so that they are even and flat.

horizontal line   an actual or imaginary line that runs across the work defining the place where sky and earth come together.

horizontal   a line or shape that is parallel to the top and bottom edges of the paper.

hue   the name of a color, such as yellow, yellow-orange, blue-violet, green.

icon   a sacred painting or image. Usually it portrays Jesus or one or more saints. Frequently done in enamel or egg tempera paint.

impressionism   a style of drawing and painting (1875 and following) begun in France, that stresses a candid glimpse of the subject, and emphasizes the momentary effects of light on color.

incised lines   very thin lines cut into the surface of a printing plate, such as in etchings or woodcuts.

jewelry   ornamental objects to be worn: rings, earrings, pendants, necklaces, bracelets.

kiln (ceramic)   an oven-like piece of equipment used to fire clay objects at high temperatures.

kneading   a technique used to prepare clay. Air is removed from the clay to obtain uniform consistency.

landscape   a work of art that shows the features of the natural environment (trees, lakes, mountains, flowers).

line   an element of design that may be two-dimensional (pencil or paper), three-dimensional (wire or rope) or implied (the edge of a shape or form).

linoleum cut   a relief print made from a piece of linoleum. The areas and lines that are cut out will remain unprinted. The original surface will transfer ink to the paper.

loom   equipment used in weaving. There are many types, from a simple cardboard loom to a four-heddle floor loom.

medium   a material used to create artwork. Plural is media.

metropolitan region   a large settled area of dwellings and industries that includes a city and its surrounding towns, villages and suburban developments.

mirror image   the "flopped-over" picture that occurs when prints are made from linoleum, wood or metal plates. Words are printed in reverse, for example.

mixed media   a two-dimensional technique that uses more than one medium; for example, a crayon and watercolor drawing.

mobile   a movable and balanced sculpture, suspended from above, that turns and rotates as it is hit by moving air.

modeling   working with clay or other materials to form three-dimensional sculptures.

monoprint   a print in which there is only one copy created. Many techniques can be used to transfer the original design to paper, but the same design cannot be repeated.

mosaics   designs or pictures made with squarish cut shapes of glass or colored stone. Mosaics can also be made of paper, natural materials, wood or cardboard.

movement   a principle of design that refers to the arrangement of parts in a drawing to create a slow-to-fast flow of your eye through the work.

mural   a large painting, made to be permanent on a wall.

mythology   the stories told in ancient Greek and Roman cultures about their gods and goddesses. These figures still are subjects for paintings and sculptures.

nature print   a print made by rolling ink on natural objects (leaves, flowers, grass) and pressing out on paper.

negative space   the area around the objects in a painting, and the space around the solid parts of a sculpture.

Neo-Classic   a style of art (begun about 1850) in which artists worked in the styles of ancient Greece and Rome; a revival of classic styles.

Nonobjective art   art with no recognizable subject matter. The real subject is the composition of the drawing or painting itself.

Op Art (Optical Art)   a style of art (mid–twentieth century) that uses optical (visual) illusions of many types. These works of art are composed to confuse, heighten or expand visual sensations.

opaque   material that will not let light pass through; the opposite of transparent.

organic   free form, or a quality that resembles living things; the opposite of mechanical or geometric.

painterly quality   that aspect of artwork that allows brushstrokes to show and let us see what the artist's movements were.

paper pulp   modeling material made by mixing small bits of paper in water and wheat paste.

papier-mâché   a technique for working with paper (strips or pulp) and glue or paste, to form three-dimensional sculptures or reliefs. It produces a solid material that is quite strong when dry.

pattern   a principle of design. Combinations of lines, colors and shapes are used to show real or imaginary things. Also achieved by repeating a shape, line or color.

perspective drawing   a method of drawing on a flat surface (which is two-dimensional) to give the illusion of depth, or the third dimension.

piers   heavy squarish columns that are the major supports for a dome or roof.

Plasticine   an oil-based clay, used for modeling. It usually stays workable and does not dry out.

Pop Art   a style of art that features the everyday, popular things around us. A drawing of a large Coke bottle might be considered Pop Art.

portrait   a piece of artwork featuring a person, several people or an animal. Portraits are usually facial, but can also be full figure.

positive space   the objects in a work of art, not the background or the space around them.

poster   a graphic design created for the purpose of promoting or selling a product or announcing an event.

Post-Impressionism   style of art that immediately followed the Impressionists in France. Cézanne was a leader of this style which stressed more substantial subjects and methods than those used by the Impressionists.

preliminary sketch   a planning sketch, usually on a small scale, to determine the basic arrangement of a design or larger work of art.

printmaking   any of several techniques for making multiple copies of a single image. Some examples are woodcuts, etchings, collagraphs and silk-screen prints.

product designer   artist who designs and gives style to manufactured products such as appliances, toys, automobiles, lighting, furniture.

proportion   a comparative size relationship between several objects or between the parts of a single object or person. In drawing, for example, get the correct relationship between the sizes of the head and body.

radial balance   a design based on a circle with the features radiating from a central point.

Realism   a style of art that realistically shows actual places, people or objects. It stresses actual colors, textures, shadows and arrangements.

relief   the raised parts of a surface that are often noticeable by the feeling of texture.

relief sculpture   a three-dimensional sculpture designed to be viewed from one side. Usually it is placed on a wall.

Renaissance   a period of time (1400–1600) following the Middle Ages. It emphasized human beings, their environment, science and philosophy. A renewal of Greek and Roman thinking regarding art and humanity.

resist   drawing and painting technique that relies on the fact that wax or oil will resist water, causing it to move to clean areas.

rhythm   a principle of design that indicates a type of movement in an artwork or design, often by repeated shapes or colors.

Rococo   a style of art (1700s) following the Baroque. It featured decorative and elegant themes and style.

Roman arch   same as the true arch. An arch with a rounded top (half circle). It was first used extensively by the ancient Romans.

Roman Art   the architecture and art of the ancient Roman peoples.

Romanesque Art   the style of architecture and art of western and southern Europe in the eleventh and twelfth centuries; usually related to churches and religious art.

Romanticism   a style of painting (mid–nineteenth century) that featured adventure, action, imagination and an interest in foreign happenings and people.

rubbing   a technique that transfers surface texture to paper by placing the paper over the textured surface and rubbing the top of the paper with a crayon or pencil.

sculpture   a carving, construction, casting or modelled form done in three-dimensions, height, width and depth.

seascape   a drawing or painting that features part of the sea as subject matter, often a coastal environment.

serigraph   a print (same as a silk-screen print) that is made by forcing ink through a stencil and silk-screen to paper below.

set-up   a group of objects arranged to be drawn or painted. A still life grouping.

shading   using two-dimensional medium to create darkened areas (shadows) that produce a feeling of space and depth.

shape   an element of design described as two-dimensional and enclosing area. Shape can be divided into two basic classes: geometric (square, triangle, circle) and organic (irregular in outline).

shaped canvas   a twentieth-century painting technique in which the canvas ground (surface) is not flat, but has objects placed behind it to form a relief surface.

silk-screen print   same as serigraph.

sketch a quick drawing that catches the immediate feeling of action or the impression of a place. Probably not a completed drawing, but may be a reference for later work.

space an element of design that indicates areas in a drawing (positive and negative) and/or the feeling of depth in a two-dimensional work of art.

stained glass the brightly colored pieces of glass used in windows and held together with strips of lead. First used in churches of the Romanesque times.

still life an arrangement of inanimate objects to draw or paint. Also, a drawing or painting of a set-up.

stitchery a textile technique in which the design is created on cloth with a variety of stitches.

street painting mural paintings done by nonprofessional artists. Usually they are painted on store sides, freeway retaining walls or fences.

subject matter the things about which the artist is communicating in a work of art.

subtle the delicate appearance or gradual change contained in a work of art. Hardly noticeable, unless a person looks carefully.

Super Realism a style of drawing and painting in the late twentieth century that emphasizes photographic realism. The objects may be greatly enlarged, yet keep their photographic appearance.

surface decorating techniques for creating designs on the surface of clay objects.

Surrealism a style of twentieth-century painting in which the artists link normally unrelated objects and situations. Often the scenes are dreamlike or set in unnatural surroundings.

symmetrical balance a design with one half that is a mirror-image of the other half.

technique any method of working with materials.

textiles objects made with cloth or fibrous materials.

texture an element of design that refers to the surface quality (rough, smooth, soft). Texture can be actual or implied.

three-dimensional materials materials such as clay, plaster, wood, metal and yarns, used to create forms that have three dimensions.

three dimensions height, width and depth. A vase has three dimensions; a picture of it has only two dimensions.

tie-bleach similar to tye-dye. Tied cloth is immersed in bleach to remove exposed color.

tie-dye a textile design technique in which the design is created by tying the cloth and immersing in dye.

traditional art any style of art that treats the subject matter in a natural (rather realistic) way. A style similar to those used for many years.

transparent the quality of an object or paper that allows objects to be seen clearly through it, such as cellophane.

true arch same as Roman arch. An arch with a semicircular top.

two-dimensional materials materials such as paints, chalks and inks that are generally used on flat surfaces.

unity a principle of design that relates to the sense of oneness or wholeness in a work of art.

urban areas parts of cities where trade and commerce, business and industry are conducted. Educational, recreational and cultural interests are woven into the lifestyle of the people living in urban areas.

value an element of design that relates to the lightness and darkness of a color or shade.

vertical upright and parallel to the sides of the paper or canvas. A standing tree is vertical.

visual environment everything that surrounds you, usually divided into two groupings: the natural environment (trees, flowers, water, sky, rocks) and the manufactured or built environment (buildings, roads, bridges, automobiles).

warp fibrous material (yarn) interlaced vertically with the horizontal weft in a weaving.

wash ink or watercolor paint that is diluted with water to make it lighter in value and more transparent.

weaving the interlacing of threads and other materials to create a textile design as an integral part of cloth.

wedging a technique in which clay is cut and slammed together several times to remove air bubbles and to produce an even texture in the clay.

wedging board equipment used to wedge clay.

weft horizontal threads in a weaving.

wet clay clay that can be fired in a kiln when it is dry.

woodcut a type of relief print, pulled from a block of wood whose surface has been cut and gouged to create the design.

Index

A

Abstract art, 87, 88
Abstract Expressionism, 91
Acropolis, 69
Action, 162, 163
Action painting, 91
Activities, suggested, 19, 27, 35, 45, 52, 66, 67, 94, 95, 106
Advertising art, 25, 26, 215–225
African art, 98, 99
Albers, Josef, 56, 93
American Indian art, 101, 102
Amézcua, Consuelo, 101
Ancient art, 68, 69, 70
Architect, 36, 37, 38
Architecture, 11, 36–41, 65
Armstrong, Roger, 30, 55
Art and commerce, 28–45
Art around us, 8–12, 15, 16
Art careers, 20–45
Art director, 25, 29
Art history, 68–95
Art understanding, 53–67
Asian art, 97, 98
Assemblage, 203
Audubon, John James, 82
Automobile design, 105

B

Balance, 61, 62, 215
Baroque art, 78–81
Batik, 55
Bauhaus, 89
Bearden, Romare, 99
Bellardo, Paul, 235
Benin art, 98
Bernini, Lorenzo, 78, 79
Bill, Max, 92, 95
Bisque, 237
Black African art, 98, 99
Botticelli, Sandro, 75
Boucher, Francois, 81
Breuer, Marcel, 40
Brommer, Gerald F., 60
Browning, Colleen, 48, 102
Bruegel, Pieter, 77
Brunelleschi, 75

Brushes, 114
Burgee, John, 37
Byzantine art, 72

C

Calder, Alexander, 205
Calligraphy, 132, 133, 222
Camera, 104
Canavier, Elena, 196
Caravaggio, 79
Cardboard prints, 184, 185
Careers in art, 20–45
Cartoon, 13, 30, 55
Cassatt, Mary, 64, 84, 150
Castoro, Rosemary, 102
Cathedral, 72, 73, 74
Catlett, Elizabeth, 98
Cave painting, 139
Ceramics, 196, 198, 228, 230, 231, 233–239
Cézanne, Paul, 85, 87, 146
Chalk, 111
Channel prints, 189
Charcoal, 111
Chardin, Jean Baptiste, 81
Chartres, Notre Dame, 74
Chase, Steve, and Associates, 43
Chicago, Judy, 93, 102, 103
Chinese art, 97, 98
Christian art, 72
Christo, 51
Close, Chuck, 171
Closson, Nanci B., 47, 168
Coiling technique, 238
Collage, 87, 144, 159
Color, 58, 59, 60, 148, 149, 223
Color wheel, 59
Colosseum, 71
Combine-Painting, 92, 166
Comics, 13, 30, 55
Commercial art, 28–35
Commercial artist, 24, 28–35
Computer art, 104, 109
Conceptual art, 98
Constable, John, 82
Construction, 203–209
Constructivism, 89
Contemporary art, 92–94

Contour drawing, 110
Contrast, 63, 64
Cool art, 92
Corot, Camille, 82
Cottingham, Robert, 105, 151, 169
Courbet, Gustave, 82
Crafts, 20, 26, 27, 226–247
Craftspeople, 26, 27
Crawford, Edith, 232
Crayon etching, 134, 135
Crayon, wax, 111, 112
Creating art, 107 ff.
Creativity, 20–23
Cubism, 87
Cultural influences, 96–106
Curci, Gregory, 53

D

Dali, Salvadore, 91
David, Jacques-Louis, 82
da Vinci, Leonardo, 75, 108, 138
Davis, Stuart, 88
Degas, Edgar, 84
De Kooning, Elaine, 162
De Kooning, Willem, 90, 91
Delacroix, Eugène, 82, 83
Derain, André, 88
Design
    Commercial, 24
    elements of, 15, 54–60, 67, 149
    Fashion, 34, 35
    Industrial, 24
    in painting, 149
    Interior, 25, 41, 42, 43
    Landscape, 44, 45
    Poster, 215–225
    principles of, 15, 61–67, 149
    suggestions, 116, 146, 178, 179, 194, 195, 227
Designers, 24 ff
Diebenkorn, Richard, 150
Donatello, 75
Drawing, 108–137
Duccio, 75
Dufy, Raoul, 88
Dürer, Albrecht, 77, 109, 174

E
Eakins, Thomas, 82
Ebelacker, Virginia, 102
Edwards, Joel, 17
Egyptian art, 68, 69
Egyptian paste, 230
Elements of design, 54–60
El Greco, 79
Emphasis, 64, 216
Emotions in art, 82, 83, 88
Environment, painting the, 188, 189
Experimental painting, 170, 171, 172, 173
Experimental printmaking, 188, 189
Expressionistic art, 82, 88, 89
Eye level, 128, 129

F
Fashion design, 34, 35
Fauvism, 89
Feitelson, Lorser, 92
Fiber art, 239–247
Fiber-tipped markers, 115
Fine art, 20, 23, 46–52
Firing clay, 237
Fish, Janet, 7, 62, 102, 149
Flack, Audrey, 102, 104
Ford, Betty Davenport, 64, 192, 196
Form, 56, 124, 125
Fragonard, Jean, 81
Francesca, Piero della, 75
Frankenthaler, Helen, 102

G
Gabo, Naum, 89
Gainsborough, Thomas, 81
Gatto, Joseph, 27, 229
Gauguin, Paul, 87
Gericault, Theodore, 82
Giacometti, Alberto, 95
Gibilterra, Charles, 33
Gill, Gene, 52
Giotto, 75
Gothic art, 74, 75
Gomez, Glynn, 101
Goya, Francisco, 81
Graphic design, 28, 29, 212–225
Graphic designer, 24
Greek art, 69, 70
Green, Martin, 187
Gris, Juan, 156
Grooms, Red, 202

H
Hagia Sophia, 73
Hammersley, Frederick, 149
Hanson, Duane, 16, 17, 106

Hand building, 232–234, 238, 239
Hard Edge Painting, 92
Harnett, William, 84, 156
Hartigan, Grace, 91
Hartley, Corrine, 35
Harunobu, Susuki, 97
Hendricks, Barkley L., 98
Hiroshige, Ando, 97, 174, 175
History of art, 68–95
Hoffman, Hans, 91
Hogarth, William, 81
Hokusai, 97
Holbein, Hans, 77
Homer, Winslow, 82, 83, 142
Hopper, Edward, 147
Hudson River School, 82
Hyde, Doug, 49, 102

I
Icon, 72
Illuminated manuscript, 73
Imagination, 164, 165, 166
Impressionism, 84–87
Indian, American, 101, 102
Industrial design, 24, 31, 32, 33, 34
Ingres, Jean Dominique, 82
Ink drawing, 113
Interior design, 25, 41, 42, 43

J
Japanese art, 97
Jewelry, 229–233
John Hancock Center, 37
Johns, Jasper, 65, 93
Johnson, Phillip, 37
Johnson, Sargent, 20, 98

K
Kandinsky, Wassily, 88
Kelly, Ellsworth, 92
Kingman, Dong, 47, 97, 98
Klee, Paul, 91
Kline, Franz, 91
Krasner, Lee, 91, 102

L
Landscape design, 44, 45
Landscape painting, 160, 161
Layout design, 10, 212–225
Le Sportsac, 28
Lettering, 132, 133, 222
Lewis, Lucy, 102
Lichtenstein, Roy, 93
Line, 54, 55, 56, 120, 121
Linoleum cuts, 178–179
Liu, Katherine Chang, 189

Living space, designing, 36–45
Logos, 137
Lonewolf, Joseph, 102
Looms, 240, 241
Lundeberg, Helen, 92

M
Maloof, Sam, 26
Manet, Edouard, 84
Marisol, 102
Markers, 115
Martinez, Julian, 102
Martinez, Maria, 14, 102, 228
Masaccio, 75
Masks, 98
Matisse, Henri, 88, 89
McIntosh, Harrison, 27, 227
Mehrinfar, Said, 42
Mexican art, 100, 101
Michelangelo, 75, 77, 108, 191
Middle Ages, art of, 72, 73, 74
Millet, Jean Francois, 82
Miro, Joan, 91
Miss, Mary Ann, 12
Mitchell, Joan, 91
Mixed-media, 144
Modeling, 196, 197, 198
Modigliani, Amedeo, 98
Moller chair, 60
Mondrian, Piet, 88
Monet, Claude, 84, 85
Monoprinting, 186, 187
Moore, Henry, 17
Movement, 66, 218, 219
Multiple originals, 174
Museums, 12

N
Nagatani, Patrick, 98
Natzler, Otto, 21
Navajo rug, 229
Neoclassic art, 82
Nevelson, Louise, 94, 102
Nieman, LeRoy, 148, 175
Nike of Samothrace, 70
Nineteenth century art, 81–84
Noguchi, Isamu, 98, 193
Nonobjective art, 88
Notre Dame, Paris, 74

O
O'Keeffe, Georgia, 102, 103
Oldenberg, Claes, 93, 195
Op Art, 168, 169
Open space, 221
Oriental art, 97, 98
Orozco, José Clemente, 101

P

Pagliaro, Carla, 170
Painting, 138–175
Pajaud, William, 155
Paper jewelry, 230
Paper sculpture, 206, 207
Papier-mâché, 199–202
Parker, Richard, 109
Parthenon, 69
Pattern, 65, 126, 127
Pei, I. M., 21, 98
Pen and ink, 113
Pencils, 111
People, painting, 152–155
Perspective, 128, 129, 130, 131
Peterson, Robert (Design), 32, 33, 42
Picasso, Pablo, 87, 95, 98
Pinch pots, 236, 238
Plasticine, 197
Pluralism, 51
Pollock, Jackson, 91
Ponce de Leon, Michael, 101
Pop Art, 92, 93, 168, 169
Posters, 212–225
Post-Impressionism, 84–87
Principles of design, 61–67
Printmaking, 174–189
Puppets, 62, 201
Pyramids, 68, 69

Q

Quesada, Eugenio, 101, 111

R

Rankin, Lou, 194
Sanzio, Raphael, 75, 76
Rauschenberg, Robert, 92
Realist art, 82, 83
Red Starr, Kevin, 101, 102
Relief prints, 178, 179, 180–185
Relief sculpture, 190
Rembrandt, 80, 81, 95
Remington, Frederic, 84
Renaissance art, 74–79
Renoir, Auguste, 84
Reynolds, Joshua, 81
Rhythm, 66
Riley, Bridget, 102
Ringgold, Faith, 98, 102
Rivera, Diego, 100, 101
Rococo art, 79–81
Rodin, Auguste, 84, 85, 193
Rodriguez, Peter, 101
Roman art, 70, 71
Romanesque art, 72, 73
Romano, Clare, 50, 63

Romantic art, 82, 83
Rosenquist, James, 93
Roth, Emery, and Son, 39
Rouault, Georges, 88, 89
Rubbings, 126, 127
Rubens, Peter Paul, 78, 79
Russell, Charles, 84
Russo, Catherine, 103

S

Salinas, Porfirio, 101
San Ildefonso, 26
San Xavier del Bac, 100
Sargent, John Singer, 23, 84
Scandinavian design, 105
Scholder, Fritz, 103
Schwitters, Kurt, 89
Sculpture, 190–209
Secunda, Arthur, 22
Senner, Eileen, 51
Sevart, Don, 50
Sgraffito, 235
Shape, 56, 122, 123
Siqueros, David, 101
Sketchbooks, 16, 18
Skidmore, Owings and Merrill, 37, 44
Smith, David, 192
Space, 57, 128, 129, 130, 131
Sphinx, 68, 69
Stella, Frank, 92
Still life, 156–159
Stitchery, 243–246
Strand, Kerry, 109
String prints, 184, 185
Subject matter
    drawing, 118, 119
    painting, 150–175
    printmaking, 171, 176
Suger, Abbot, 75
Surface decoration, 235
Surrealism, 91
Sylwester, Roland, 63, 201
Symbols, 29

T

Tang Dynasty, 96
Tanguy, Yves, 91
Tempera paint, 140–142
Teotihuacan, 100
Techniques
    ceramics, 235–237
    painting, 144, ff.
    printmaking, 174–189
    stitchery, 243, 245
    weaving, 239–243
Textiles, 239–247

Texture, 58, 59, 60, 126, 127
Thiebaud, Wayne, 169
Three-dimensional art, 194–196
Tie-bleach, 247
Tie-dye, 246, 247
Titian, 77
Tools
    ceramics, 234
    drawing, 111–115
    painting, 140
    printmaking, 174–176
    weaving, 240–242
Toulouse-Lautrec, Henri, 87
Turner, Don LaViere, 177
Turner, William, 82
Twentieth century art, 87–92

U

Ullberg, Kent, 10, 15, 46, 191, 195, 198
Umgelter, Linda, 41
Understanding art, 53–67
Unity, 62, 63, 217

V

Value, 58, 59, 60, 124, 125
Van Dyck, Anthony, 79, 80, 112
Van Eyck, Jan, 76, 77
Van Gogh, Vincent, 86, 87
Vanishing point, 128, 129, 130
Velarde, Pablita, 102
Vermeer, Jan, 80
Vickrey, Robert, 48, 153
Vigil, Veloy, 102, 139, 153, 177

W

Warhol, Andy, 22, 93
Wash drawing, 114
Watercolor, 140, 142, 143
Watteau, Antoine, 81
Wax crayons, 111, 112
Wayne, June, 102
Weaving, 239–243
Wedging, 234
White, Charles, 99
Whistler, James McNeill, 84
Wiegmann, Richard, 110
Wire sculpture, 203, 204, 205
Women in art, 102, 103
Wong, Tyrus, 98
Wood construction, 208, 209
Woodcut, 180, 181, 183, 184
Wood jewelry, 232
Wood, Robert E., 18
Wyeth, Andrew, 57, 61

Acknowledgments

Gathering the visual material to produce a book such as this is a co-operative effort that involves many people. We would like to express our thanks to the following art teachers and supervisors for providing illustrative materials for the book: Marge Broadhurst, Gerald Citrin, Laura DeWyngaert, Joseph Gatto, Nancy Guenther, Rueben Jaramillo, Thomas A. Jambro, J. D. Kain, Bebe Kearney, Nancy Kinne, Audrey Kraake, Gary Langer, Helen Liutjens, Thomas Nielson, Ann Plauzoles, Louise Romito, Mary Ryan, Jack Selleck, Margaret Sikes, Roland Sylwester, Natsu Tomimatsu, Alice Turner, Michael Violante, Norma Wrege, and Jack Yoshimi. And we also wish to thank their students for creating such excellent examples for us to use.

The following artists and collectors graciously granted permission to reprint their works in this book: Roger Armstrong, Romare Bearden, Paul Bellardo, Colleen Browning, Elena Canavier, Judy Chicago, Christo, Chuck Close, Nanci B. Clossen, Robert Cottingham, Elaine de Kooning, Willem de Kooning, Joel Edwards, Janet Fish, Betty Davenport Ford, Joseph Gatto, Gene Gill, Martin Green, Red Grooms, Frederick Hammersley, Duane Hanson, Corrine Hartley, Jasper Johns, Dong Kingman, Katherine Chang Liu, Sam Maloof, Harrison McIntosh, Mary Ann Miss, Henry Moore, Otto Natzler, LeRoy Nieman, Isamu Noguchi, Claes Oldenburg, Carla Pagliaro, Richard Parker, William Pajaud, Eugenio Quesada, Lou Rankin, Clare Romano, Fritz Scholder, Arthur Secunda, Eileen Senner, Don Sevart, Kerry Strand, Wayne Thiebaud, Don LaViere Turner, Kent Ullberg, Robert Vickrey, Veloy Vigil, Richard Wiegmann and Robert E. Wood.

We are especially grateful to the staffs of the following galleries for allowing us to reproduce the work of artists they represent: Hirschl B. Adler Galleries, New York; Leo Castelli, Inc., New York; Indian Art Center of California, Studio City; Kennedy Galleries, New York; Louis K. Miesel Gallery, New York; Robert Miller Gallery, New York; Louis Newman Galleries, Beverly Hills; Orlando Gallery, Sherman Oaks, California; Pace Gallery, New York; and Treasure State Gallery, Great Falls, Montana.

We are also grateful to the staffs of the following museums for permission to reproduce works in their collections: Albertina Museum, Vienna; Baltimore Museum of Art, Maryland; British Museum, London; Capitoline Museum, Rome; Dallas Museum of Fine Art, Texas; Fort Worth Museum of Art, Texas; Hirshhorn Museum, Washington, D.C.; Kimbell Art Museum, Fort Worth, Texas; Los Angeles County Museum of Art, California; The Louvre, Paris; McNay Art Institute, San Antonio, Texas; Metropolitan Museum of Art, New York; Museum of Contemporary Crafts, New York; Museum of Fine Arts, Boston; Museum of Modern Art, New York; National Gallery of Art, London; National Gallery of Art, Washington, D.C.; National Museum of Anthropology, Mexico City; Norton Simon Foundation, Los Angeles; Norton Simon Museum of Art, Pasadena; Philadelphia Museum of Art, Pennsylvania; The Prado, Madrid; Rijksmuseum, Amsterdam, Holland; The Rodin Museum, Paris; Tate Gallery, London; Texas Memorial Museum, Austin; Whitney Museum of American Art, New York; and the William Rockhill Nelson Gallery of Art, Kansas City, Missouri.

We would also like to thank the following firms and governmental agencies for their cooperation in supplying visual materials for this book: Adler, Schwartz Graphics, Inc., Baltimore; Marcel Breuer, Architect, New York; CalComp, Anaheim; Steve Chase and Associates, Palm Springs; Walt Disney Productions, Burbank; Ford Motor Company; French Government Tourist Office, New York; General Motors, Inc.; Hanna Barbera, Los Angeles; Italian Tourist Office, New York; Jamison and Burgee, Architects, New York; Le Sportsac, Inc.; 3M Company, Minneapolis; Nissan Motors, Torrance; I.M. Pei, Architects, New York; Robert Peterson Design, Chicago; Emery Roth and Sons, New York; Saul Bass and Associates, Los Angeles; Scan, Baltimore; Skidmore, Owings and Merrill, New York; and Trans World Airlines, New York.

We also wish to thank the hundreds of art teachers from across the country who have encouraged us with their use of the first edition of this text. Their constant good will encouraged us to produce this second edition. Thank you.

Photo credits

Teachers from many schools across the nation supplied photos of student work for this book. We realize that students are constantly producing work that is excellent in quality and exciting in concept. The pieces reproduced in this text are used because they help expand the ideas presented in the text.

We are indebted to students from the following schools. The numbers indicate the pages on which the work is found. Baltimore Public Schools: 226, 239, 240, 241, 242, 243, 246, 249. Baseline Junior High School, Boulder, Colorado: 121, 157. California State University, Fullerton: 127, 230. Carver Junior High School, Los Angeles: 145, 159. Curtiss Junior High School, Carson, California: 160. Dodson Junior High School, San Pedro, California: 164. Emerson Junior High School, Los Angeles: 112, 133, 136, 161, 165, 167, 171, 172, 197, 208, 209. Highland School, Libertyville, Illinois: 236. Le Conte Junior High School, Hollywood, California: 207. Lutheran Junior High School, Los Angeles: 55, 58, 113, 114, 117, 119, 121, 123, 125, 127, 130, 131, 136, 140, 141, 148, 152, 157, 158, 159, 160, 163, 165, 167, 170, 172, 176, 182, 187, 199, 203, 204, 205, 207, 225, 234, 237. Mansfield State College, Pennsylvania: 231, 232. Paul Revere Junior High School, Los Angeles: 114, 115, 134, 135, 144, 224. San Diego City Schools: 244. Seoul American High School, Seoul, Korea: 55, 118, 120, 122, 126, 183, 186, 246. Stephen White Junior High School, Carson, California: 119. Thorne Junior High School, Port Monmouth, New Jersey: 154, 202. Tigard High School, Oregon: 238. Van Wyck Junior High School, Wappinger's Falls, New York: 228. Wilmington Junior High School, Wilmington, California: 167.